To Kent,
best wishes.

17.11.2000   New York

KASPAROV
AGAINST THE
WORLD

The story of the greatest
online challenge

by World Chess Champion **Garry Kasparov**
with Grandmaster Daniel King

KasparovChess Online
www.KasparovChess.com

Published by KasparovChess Online, Inc.
32 Broadway, 4th floor
New York, NY 10004
(212) 269-3400 • www.kasparovchess.com

The KasparovChess Online Team
Executive Advisor: Tom Walker
Technical Advisor: Boris Alterman
Programmers of the Computer Program "Junior": Shay Bushinsky and Amir Bonn

Produced by LifeTime Media, Inc.
352 Seventh Avenue, 15th floor
New York, NY 10001
(212) 631-7524 • Ltmedia@aol.com
• • •
President: Jacqueline Varoli
Editorial Director: Laurie Barnett
Editorial Assistant: Karin Duque
Page Designer: Chris Thomas
Jacket Design by Wendy Bass

ISBN: 0-9704813-0-6

10 9 8 7 6 5 4 3 2 1

First Edition

Printed in the United States of America

The launch for my Internet game against the World took place on June 21st, 1999, at Bryant Park in Manhattan on a strangely dark and blustery Monday morning. Rain threatened. Perhaps it was a portent of what was to come.

An open tent housed glowing computer terminals and a giant chessboard. Surrounding the board was a gaggle of chess-playing school kids and a pack of journalists, all waiting for me to make my first move. And there was Irina Krush, a Russian émigreé and now a resident of New York, one of the four analysts who would be making recommendations during the game.

In the midst of this public relations clamor it was difficult to imagine that the game would be at all serious, particularly when the most popular question among the journalists was "How long will the World last?" I have to say that I was not anticipating any particular difficulties. I was sure it would be a serious game, but I was confident that I would be able to finish matters in under forty moves.

We all said our piece for the kids and cameras. When it came to Irina's turn to speak I was slightly concerned when she stated she was proud to be playing against Garry Kasparov. I thought, "Playing Garry Kasparov? Isn't she just submitting recommendations. . . ?" It was impossible for me to foresee that Irina, with the help of her management team, would be heading a powerful group of players that would dominate the polls for forty moves, and in the process take me to the brink of defeat.

Twenty days later, Irina's words came back to me. It felt as if I had been caught in a trap.

FOREWORD

When I first heard about the idea for an interactive chess game in which Garry Kasparov would take on all comers over the Internet, I was intrigued. I wondered whether the game would prove to be a walkover for the world's greatest chess player or develop into something more interesting. I also wondered how Microsoft could help make the game a reality—MSN Gaming Zone was eager to host it, as it was already offering chess and had built a substantial audience of Internet gamers from around the world.

When the game began, I was amazed at the worldwide attention it attracted and knew that we were on to something big. The game that unfolded was not only unpararelled in the annals of chess history, it was also fascinating. The worldwide chess community executed a breathtakingly risky and complex strategy, forcing Kasparov into a complicated endgame that moved the game beyond the comprehension of most of us casual chess players.

This high-profile game introduced millions to the ability of the Internet to entertain, educate, and energize people from around the world and united them for a single purpose: to challenge the world's best chess player. The combination of interactive technology with the ancient game of chess transcended geographic, cultural, and language barriers. As you read about this groundbreaking event, step back and consider the broader potential of the technology. It truly is mind-boggling.

Microsoft is proud to have sponsored such a successful interactive chess event, and I'd like to take this opportunity to thank everyone involved. The World Team should be commended for playing such a superb game, and for providing countless hours of fascination and learning for chess fans around the world. And Garry should be congratulated for winning the "Microsoft Match" and bringing such a great idea to fruition.

—Bill Gates, 2000

INTRODUCTION

I had originally discussed the idea of playing an Internet game against the World in 1997, after my second match against the computer, Deep Blue. My friend, Fred Friedel, who had first introduced me to computers in 1985, had an idea to conduct the match from Germany in connection with the magazine *Der Spiegel*, but *Kasparov Against the World* never went beyond the planning stage. Nevertheless, I was intrigued by the concept.

I was interested in setting up my own chess website—it has recently been launched as KasparovChess Online (KCO)—but I really had no idea what kind of worldwide audience I could hope to attract. During my matches with Deep Blue, there had been a phenomenal number of people following the games on the Internet, but it was difficult to know whether they were interested in computers, chess, or just watching me trip myself up. It was important for me to get an idea of potential numbers to reassure myself—and potential investors—of the worth of the site. Therefore, I returned to the idea of having a long-term chess event on the Internet, this time in cooperation with a major multi-national computer corporation, so as to identify an audience and to find out how best to work with it.

No matter what you want to do on the Internet, you need a powerful partner, so my agent, Owen Williams, and I began by going to the largest computer company in the business: Microsoft. We figured that only a company with its resources would be able to work with a large global audience and, if necessary, be able to remedy any problems that might occur during the event. In view of the huge undertaking, I had no doubt there would be mistakes, but with Microsoft's back-up, I was confident there would be few errors and the consequences would be minimized. That was in the late Autumn of 1998. It didn't take long for them to come back with a positive response.

We finalized the whole concept in Seattle in April 1999. Microsoft's main concern was that the game could turn into a disaster: No one would look good if the World lost its queen on move 15; and Microsoft would not get the lengthy exposure it was looking for to build up traffic on its MSN portal. To avoid that possibility I suggested that there should be four analysts who would make recommendations before each move. With their guidance, it would be unlikely that the World would make any gross blunders.

The next question was whom to invite. I did not want the game to turn into a grudge contest with a rival top Grandmaster—I have enough of that in my regular tournaments—so we decided to gather four teenage players, the next generation of chess masters. The strongest of the four was 16-year-old Etienne Bacrot from France, who, two years before, had become one of the world's youngest Grandmasters. The others were 19-year-old Florin Felecan from Chicago, a recent émigré from Romania; 14-year-old Elisabeth Paehtz, a member of the German women's team—I had been impressed by her in an exhibition match we played at the Hannover computer trade fair in March 1999; and Irina Krush, at 15 already the U.S. women's champion. And as an extra safeguard, there would be an event moderator, Grandmaster Danny King from England, who would not make recommendations, but instead would explain the play in the game.

A detailed cycle of play was conceived. This was not the easiest of tasks, as schedules had to be coordinated between different time zones, but in the end it was worked out to everyone's satisfaction. I would have twelve hours to decide upon my move. The deadline for submitting it to Microsoft in Seattle would be 6 PM Pacific Standard Time (PST). My move would then be communicated to the coaches, who would have twelve hours, until 6 AM PST, to decide on their move recommendations. The recommendations and commentary would then be edited (and sometimes translated) and posted, together with my move, at 12 noon PST on the game site. At 12 noon, the World would start voting. Anyone could log on to the Microsoft Gaming Zone and vote; it was simply the move that received the greatest number of votes that was played. The World had a total of eighteen hours in which to vote, finishing at 6 AM PST the following day. The move that received the most votes would then be posted, and I would have twelve hours to decide on my next move—and the cycle would repeat. This full cycle would take forty-eight hours. In other words, one move was going to be made every day.

On paper, the cycle might seem a little convoluted, but it didn't take long to get used to the routine. After a few weeks, no matter where I was in the world, my body clock was running in time with the game. For four months it was something from which I could not escape.

As I said above, my declared intention was to use the game as a piece of market research: I wanted to figure out what kind of a world audience there was for chess. I was sincere when I stated to journalists before the launch of the game in June, "This is an experiment about the potential of the Internet. The big difference with my match against Deep Blue is that this is not about winning or losing." How wrong I was. It ended up being exactly about that: winning or losing. It is curious how the true nature of chess always comes through: It is a struggle, it is a fight with an opponent. Before the game I thought I was the favorite to win; it could possibly be a draw, but I didn't think I could lose. A month after the start of the game, I thought otherwise. I was under pressure, and I had to fight. It is in my nature. That is what it means to be a chess player.

In our preparatory discussions with Microsoft in Seattle, the last thing that any of us anticipated was that the game would turn out to be a long, high-quality, professional struggle that would consume most of my time over the summer and autumn. I am not sure I would have taken it on if I had thought that was going to happen. It is true that in the end I did not play my scheduled world championship match against Viswanathan Anand in October 1999, but with the amount of time I devoted to this single game against the World, and the prolonged tension of the struggle, it felt as though I had been through a world championship match.

I went into this game a little naively. Naturally, it had occurred to me that the world coaches could have the support of stronger players, and of course, the back-up of powerful computers. However, I thought this would be balanced by the fact that they would have to work together as a team. In a game like chess, where consistent, single-minded strategy is so crucial to success, it was hard for me to imagine that a committee of players could ever mount a serious challenge to me.

I have had some previous experience of this kind of consultation game. In Bordeaux in 1993, I gave a simultaneous exhibition where one of the boards was taken by MiniTel, the French telecommunications system. Just as in this Microsoft game, anyone could log on and discuss the situation, then a vote was taken for each move, and the operator physically played out the "winning" move on the board. After just a few moves the MiniTel participants had managed to blunder away a crucial pawn, and they lost quickly. I joked that the game confirmed "the inefficiency of collective ownership." Perhaps I spoke too soon. As the simultaneous exhibition was only just beginning, I decided to give them another chance. In the second game they played much better, thanks to some decent club players who dominated the discussions on the MiniTel site and started insisting on moves. In fact, it was a hard struggle to overcome my opponents. But not even that experience warned me of the trouble I was to encounter in the game against the World.

I underestimated the enormous power and potential of the Internet for bringing people together and the way in which Irina and Smart Chess, her management company, would eventually manage to win over the World Team to their cause. With the perspective of hindsight, it was a remarkable achievement, and I have to praise Ron Henley, the manager of the Smart Chess team, for his splendid work. He put together a great team that produced a strong performance. Naturally, his principal aim was to promote his website and his client, Irina Krush, but it resulted in the creation of a wonderful game of chess.

It is difficult to say who the World Team's strongest adviser was, particularly when the Internet, and the nature of the game, granted anonymity to anyone who wished to maintain it. And, quite frankly, it seemed to me there were a lot of people who would have liked to knock me off my pedestal. Now they had their chance. A player who never made a secret of his contributions was Alexander Khalifman. He and his Grandmaster School in St. Petersburg played a significant role in the World Team's analysis. I have great respect for Khalifman's abilities as an analyst. Judging by his contributions to opening theory, he is obviously a creative thinker and a hard worker away from the board: When I am researching sharp variations of the Sicilian or the Gruenfeld openings, his name appears with some frequency in chess theory books. At the end of July he took a temporary break from the game to take part in the World Chess Federation (FIDE) knockout tournament—in which he was victorious—and it came as quite a relief to me.

But it was not just a question of a few strong chess players combining their intellects to challenge me. What was unique about this event was that as well as just voting for a move, anyone could participate in the creative process that went into selecting the next move. The bulletin boards on the MSN Gaming Zone were the forum where this real time discussion took place. Chess experts led the debate, but many less experienced players contributed valuable ideas, very much in the democratic spirit of the Internet; moreover, such an open discussion ensured that everyone stayed in touch with the latest thinking on the game, thus unifying the World Team when it came to the crucial vote for the move. I had thought that efficient communication was going to be one of my opponents' main problems, but, with clever organization by Smart Chess, the open forum of the bulletin boards, and the dedication of chess enthusiasts from all over the world, this potential weakness was turned into a strength. The sum of the World's efforts was greater than its parts.

Yuri Dokhoian

There were chiefly two people who assisted me in my analysis of the game: Yuri Dokhoian and Boris Alterman. Yuri is 35 years old. He grew up in Siberia, but now lives in Moscow and has been my full-time coach since November 1994. We hadn't known each other at all before then, but he came highly recommended to me—and I have to be very grateful for that recommendation. He is a great coach and has become a great friend. Yuri's character is a good match for mine—he is steady, solid, and calm. In the past I used to prepare for major events with three or four people, but now it is just Yuri who assists me. He accompanies me to these events, too. I feel far more comfortable when it is just the two of us working together.

It was only in mid-July, after the game had started, that I formally asked Boris Alterman to join our analysis team. I was becoming concerned about my position against the World, and I should have been preparing for my world championship match with Anand. It was necessary to bring in reinforcements. I have known Boris since 1986 when he was a teenager attending my classes at the legendary Botvinnik chess school in Moscow. Boris takes his work seriously and is charming company. Although we are good friends now, he still addresses me by my first name and patronymic, Garry Kimovich, the Russian way of showing respect, as he did when he was my pupil at the school in Moscow. (A short digression: All Russians have three names: a given name; a patronymic—my father's name was Kim, which becomes Kimovich; and the family name. So my full name is Garry Kimovich Kasparov.)

A few years ago Boris emigrated to Israel and is a regular member of its national team. He is chess director of KasparovChess Online in Tel Aviv, so he has access to Deep Junior, which is now housed in the KCO offices.

Nowadays, when analyzing and researching a chess position, it is essential to have the assistance of a chess-playing computer. It would be a mistake to imagine that a computer can "solve" all one's chess problems. In certain strategically unbalanced positions—of which there were plenty in my game against the World, a computer's judgement is still unsophisticated. However, where straight calculation and tactics are involved, they are usually very strong. The trick is to understand when to use a computer, and how. This is a skill in itself—at which Yuri and Boris are highly proficient. They both sense whether the machine is pursuing a worthwhile continuation, or whether it should be guided in another direction.

From around halfway through the game, Deep Junior became a powerful recruit to our team. Junior was created in 1994 by two Israeli computer scientists, Shay Bushinsky and Amir Ban, and is now one of the world's strongest chess-playing programs. Deep Junior is the same basic program, but modified to run on four parallel processors. In other words, it is thinking with four brains. Shay and Amir have developed an innovative search function allowing it to calculate to an unusual depth, even by computer standards. It was particularly useful in the queen and pawn ending that developed in combination with existing endgame databases (see later for more on this), though, I should stress again, for many positions in this game, its judgement was suspect.

When we ran into trouble in the game in July, Boris would often call us in the middle of our chess work in the afternoon. For a time the refrain was nearly always the same. His low, lugubrious voice would sound across the ether: "Garry Kimovich, I have bad news, bad news." He would then tell us of his latest discoveries, most of which did nothing to brighten our moods. Yuri, Boris, and I complemented each other well in our personalities and styles of play: Yuri was determined, while Boris sounded a note of caution if my optimism ran away with me. We made an excellent team.

The main people handling the project at Microsoft were Eddie Ranchigoda, product manager at the Gaming Zone, and Diane McDade, PR manager for MSN. I would like to express my thanks to them for all their hard work, which helped to make the event such a success. And it was a success. *Kasparov Against the World* was the largest ever interactive gaming event, attracting over 3 million visitors from seventy-five different countries around the globe, with a total of 28 million page views. There were 58,000 voters during the game. This last figure is perhaps the only blemish on the statistics: Although it is an excellent figure, it was perhaps a little disappointing in view of the total number of spectators. This is the future challenge for KasparovChess Online—to convert those passive observers into active participants. Perhaps some people felt ill-qualified to vote due to the complex nature of the game. Still, Microsoft was certainly delighted by the figures at the end of the game. Its aim was to generate more traffic on the MSN Gaming Zone site, and in that it succeeded very well. Bill Gates, the president of Microsoft, learned that we had received phenomenal worldwide publicity following the launch, and I received a personal e-mail from him wishing me well in the struggle.

The following account is purely my version of events that took place in the game—others have already had their say. I have described how I was thinking at the time, and why I came to make certain decisions. If you are interested in an even more detailed chess analysis, I have produced a CD of the game that can be obtained from the KasparovChess Online website. It contains variations in ChessBase format with a brief overview, highlighting the critical moments of the game. This book gives the story behind the game, too.

As the game progressed, it consumed more and more of my time, so it is unsurprising that my other activities were affected—and vice-versa. Therefore, the game has been written in diary form, showing the move played on the day; the analysts' recommendations; exactly how many votes the top five moves obtained (on average around forty different moves received votes on each turn); and where I was on that day. When relevant I have mentioned what I was doing in my life at the time and how it fit in with the struggle on the chess board.

It turned out to be a remarkable game and a dramatic few months for me. I hope this book recaptures some of the atmosphere of that time.

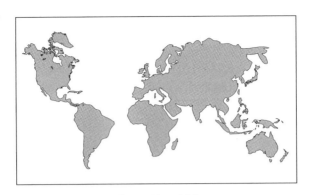

BLACK—THE WORLD

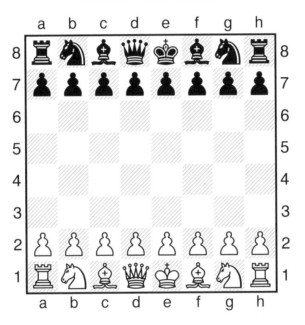

WHITE—Garry Kasparov

21ST JUNE

NEW YORK

1 e4

Accompanied by massive worldwide publicity, the game got underway in New York. I didn't go into this game completely unprepared. Together with my trainer, Yuri Dokhoian, I took the precaution of looking at the openings of the four analysts. With White they all played 1 d4, so, with little hesitation. I decided to play 1 e4 on the first move—perhaps they would find themselves in territory that was a little unfamiliar. Besides, I liked the symbolism of playing my king's pawn two squares forward: It is the king's move; it was fitting.

22ND JUNE

WASHINGTON, D.C., THEN BACK TO NEW YORK

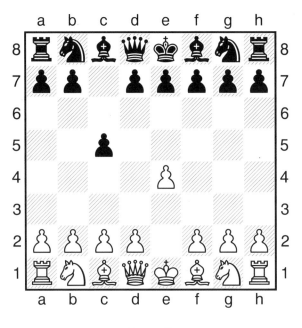

1...c5

> **Analysts' Recommendations:** Krush 1...c5; Paehtz 1...c5; Felecan 1...d6; Bacrot 1...c5.
>
> **Voting Results:** 1...c5, 2,270; 1...e5, 1,548; 1...d6, 584; 1...e6 222; 1...Nf6 192.

With three of the four analysts recommending **1...c5**, it was perhaps no surprise that this pawn move topped the poll, ousting **1...e5**, the more traditional response to my first move. The vote was merely reflecting the current trend in modern chess: At top levels, the Sicilian Defense is the most commonly played opening with Black.

The Sicilian Defense, introduced with 1...c5, has a reputation for being a lively counter-attacking opening, which it certainly would live up to in this game. This is my favorite opening when playing with Black, so, for the moment, it was as though I was playing against myself.

The next morning we were all off on the early morning shuttle to Washington, D.C., for a second version of the launch. The atmosphere there was the same as New York: children, journalists, and one interview after another. There was not one person who was taking this game seriously. "What about Deep Blue? Deep Blue was your real opponent. This is just fun!" was the standard cry. This was everything but a professional game of chess, and, to a certain extent, I was taken in by it all.

The PR for these kind of events is a necessary chore, but, in this case, it was particularly difficult as I was having problems getting my basic message across. Typically, in a three-minute interview, the first question would be about my 1997 match with Deep Blue, the second would concern Russian politics, and then there would be little time to talk about the Microsoft game. For that reason I thought it was pointless doing short interview slots on the east coast morning TV shows. A few nights before I had appeared on the "Charlie Rose Show," which followed exactly the same pattern; however, that was an interview that ran over twenty minutes, so there was enough time to discuss the Microsoft game.

After the press conference was over, I had a little time to meet some personal friends on Capitol Hill, and then it was straight back to New York.

23RD JUNE

NEW YORK TO ZURICH

2 Nf3

I didn't need to think too much about this move. I replied in the standard fashion, bringing out my knight so that it influenced the center of the board.

24TH JUNE

ZURICH

2...d6

> **Analysts' Recommendations:** Krush 2...d6; Paehtz 2...d6; Felecan 2...d6; Bacrot 2...d6.
>
> **Voting Results:** 2...d6 4,665; 2...Nc6 1,117; 2...Nf6 694; 2...e6 331; 2...d5 102.

2...d6 is the most flexible move at this point. The vast majority of top-class games now continue **3 d4** leading, after 3...cxd4 4 Nxd4, to an open game, and one of the most heavily analyzed positions in modern opening theory.

───────────────── ♜ ─────────────────

There was no time to look at chess. On my day off from the game I was guest speaker at the Bank Hoffmann annual shareholders meeting in Zurich, so I spent an hour in the morning preparing notes for my talk, and most important, resting.

In this forum I will spare you an analysis of the state of the Russian economy, but, if you are interested, you can read my articles in *The Wall Street Journal*.

I am confident when speaking about familiar subjects, but, just like playing a good game of chess, one needs energy to bring the whole thing to life. In the past I think I was in danger of diluting my energy across a variety of activities. However, I had taken a hard look at my situation three years ago, which led me to change my lifestyle. I am simply better organized than I used to be, and this enables me to achieve more, both on and off the chessboard.

25TH JUNE

ZURICH

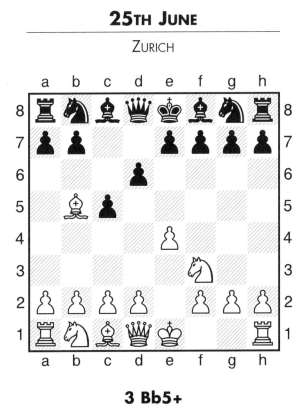

3 Bb5+

For a long time 3 Bb5+ had a reputation as a second-rate move. It was a sign that White was playing cautiously. However, over the past ten years, that view has changed. It might not be the most dangerous option in the position, but when Alexei Shirov and Vassily Ivanchuk, two of the most talented players of the younger generation, were prepared to play it against me for a win, I discovered there was more to the check than is apparent at first glance. Moreover, since Vladimir Kramnik introduced some new ideas for White in his match against Gelfand in 1994, there has been renewed interest in this line. If both players play the opening in the right spirit, then the game can become very exciting. 3 Bb5+ changes the nature of the struggle. There will not be an immediate clash as after 3 d4, but there are enough options for an aggressive fight.

Besides, I did not want to play the standard **3 d4**. That could easily lead to the Najdorf variation of the Sicilian Defense—3…cxd4 4 Nxd4 Nf6 5 Nc3 a6 —one of my favorite openings with Black.

What would I do against it? White has a variety of reasonable options on this sixth move: 6 Bc4; 6 Be2; 6 f4; 6 g3; 6 Be3; 6 Bg5—and, with the exception of the last, I have played them all. The problem is, to make this choice, I would have to look at all the possible consequences of my decision, including which part of my openings research I was prepared to reveal. This complicated search would arrive at move six, right in the middle of a high pressure event: the Frankfurt Giants speed tournament. Immersed in a draining competitive atmosphere, I would not want the distraction of such a big decision. It might be suicidal for my chances in the Frankfurt tournament.

From left to right: Garry Kasparov; chess commentator Helmut Pfleger; and Vishy Anan.

Moreover, the Najdorf could well be one of the battlegrounds in my forthcoming world title match with Vishy Anand, so I had no desire to get involved in a public theoretical duel, even though I was sure I could find something unpleasant for my opponents.

My plan was to try to avoid any critical decisions before July 12th. By that time I would be in the calm atmosphere of my summer training camp in Croatia with my trainer, Yuri Dokhoian, and a powerful computer at our side. With 3 Bb5+, at the very least, I would have enough "automatic" moves to make before heading back to Moscow.

In the meantime, I had to think about the Siemens-sponsored Frankfurt Giants. With opponents like Vishy Anand and Vladimir Kramnik, respectively rated number 2 and 3 in the World, and Anatoly Karpov, my old world championship rival, I could not afford to be below my best. I certainly didn't want to repeat the disastrous start I had had in Frankfurt the year before when I lost to Kramnik and Anand in the first two rounds.

It had been a little while since my last serious game—Sarajevo at the end of May—so it was important for me to get some practice before Frankfurt. I wanted to play some speed chess (25 minutes per player per game) with someone, so, as I was in Switzerland, a four-game match was arranged with one of its top players, Yannick Pelletier, a Grandmaster. It was kept secret by the people who arranged it, and I had the guarantee that none of the games would be published.

From my point of view the score was perfect, though I have to say I didn't play very convincingly. Nevertheless, I was happy to get some practice after a break; and we had some theoretically interesting openings.

26TH JUNE

ZURICH

3...Bd7

Analysts' Recommendations: Krush, 3...Nd7; Paehtz, 3...Nd7; Felecan, 3...Bd7; Bacrot, 3...Bd7.

Voting Results: 3...Bd7, 3,119; 3...Nd7, 2,127; 3...Nc6, 662; 3...Kb5, 143; 3...a6, 23.

Meanwhile, back at the game, I was delighted to see Irina and Elisabeth opting for 3...Nd7. Although I have played this move myself, I don't think it would have been a good choice for the World in this kind of game: White has too many interesting options available. With the knight on d7 causing a temporary blockage, Black must play with great precision if development is to be completed successfully. I know from my own experience how difficult Black's task can be—I once lost a game against Ivanchuk in this line. Moreover, it would not be easy to explain the complexities of Black's strategy to the other players online.

I always used to play 3...Nd7 against 3 Bb5+, but, after another complex encounter, this time with Shirov in Linares 1994, I decided that 3...Bd7 had to be the right choice. It is the most straightforward move. It also symbolized a certain departure for me.

> *"...the older generation was often content to play for a draw against me... the younger generation played... to win. Their attitude was different: They no longer believed I was invincible, and as a consequence, the chess world became more interesting."*
>
> —*Garry Kasparov*

There was a time after I won the world championship title in 1985 until around 1993, when I believed I had to fight for victory at any price, with Black as well as White. And 3...Nd7 fit in with that point of view. Then the chess world changed. Whereas the older generation was often content to play for a draw against me with White, the younger generation played 3Bb5+ to win. Their attitude was different: They no longer believed I was invincible, and as a consequence, the chess world became more interesting. I realized I didn't need to provoke complications from the very outset of the game. Therefore, in 1994, I made some changes to my opening repertoire, and switching from 3...Nd7 to 3...Bd7 was one of them.

As it turned out, the boys held sway at the start of the game, and they went for **3...Bd7**. This is the real reason that 3 Bb5+ has a drawish reputation: A pair of pieces is exchanged after just four moves. Anyway, I wasn't relying on Black playing 3...Nd7. Against 3...Bd7 I already had in mind Vladimir Kramnik's set-up. Since 1994 it has become the most popular way for White to play the opening. Black's position is not in immediate danger, but there is a bewildering choice of plans available that would create practical difficulties for my opponents.

27TH JUNE

TRAVEL TO FRANKFURT

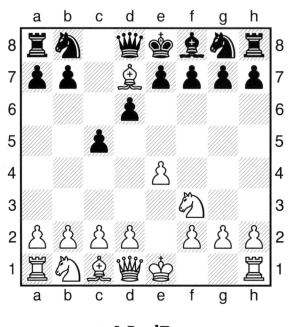

4 Bxd7+

If White is to get anything from the opening it is necessary to exchange bishops, otherwise it would take longer to bring out my remaining pieces.

I arrived in Frankfurt on Sunday, the 27th of June. The opening ceremony and banquet were on the following Monday, and play would start on Tuesday. We were to play four days in a row, with three games a day; the time control was 25 minutes per player per game. In such a long event I knew that if I survived the start, then I should be the clear favorite. My goal was "plus one" (one win and three draws, for instance) against each of my three opponents, which I thought should be enough to win the tournament.

I was very motivated in Frankfurt. I wanted to destroy the myth that I was not a good speed player. Kramnik and Anand are both excellent at speed chess, but if you look at our records, I am stronger. For instance, in the ten PCA tournaments, they both won two tournaments, and I won three. I also won two of the three Immopar speed tournaments in Paris.

I went to Frankfurt to win.

28TH JUNE

OPENING CEREMONY IN FRANKFURT

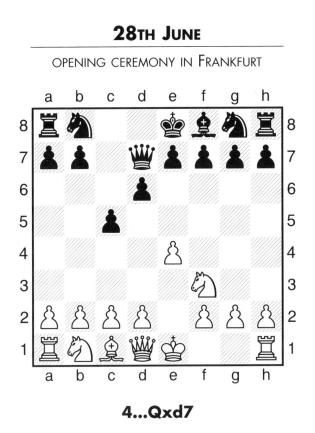

4...Qxd7

> **Analysts' Recommendations:** Krush, 4...Qxd7; Paehtz, 4...Qxd7; Felecan, 4...Qxd7; Bacrot, no recommendation for this move.
>
> **Voting Results:** 4...Qxd7, 4,479; 4...Nxd7, 1,976; 4...Kxd7, 231; 4...Nf6, 20; 4...Nc6, 12.

How one recaptures the bishop is perhaps a question of taste—I have also played **4...Nxd7** here—but I feel that **4...Qxd7** is the most natural move, preparing to bring the knight out to its best square on c6.

29TH JUNE

DAY 1 OF FRANKFURT GIANTS

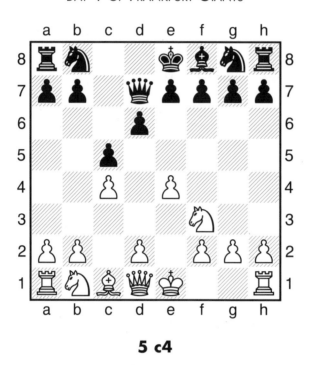

5 c4

This was an easy move to play—I was still heading for Kramnik's set-up. By playing another pawn into the middle I was looking to establish a rock-solid bind on the center.

At this point I had another inkling that there was trouble ahead. Even at this early stage Irina was producing lengthy commentaries to accompany her move recommendations on the game website. It was disconcerting, but it didn't strike me that I would soon be facing a mountain of analysis. I was immersed in the tournament, so I couldn't concern myself about the situation.

Karpov vs. Kasparov in Frankfurt

At Frankfurt, in spite of my success against Pelletier, I was still not confident about my form, so the first couple of days were crucial. To the delight of the spectators and assembled journalists, I faced Karpov in the first round—it was our first encounter in almost three years. I was less thrilled.

In the couple of years before the "Supertorneo" in Las Palmas 1996, Karpov had still been the number 2 or 3 in the world. His participation in that tournament was completely justified. However, he ended up tying for last place, having failed to win a single game, overshadowed by a new generation of players. From that time, his decline began. It is a fact that Karpov simply cannot compete as he used to at the highest levels.

I felt that as the top three players in the world had been invited to Frankfurt, it would have been appropriate to include Shirov, the number 4, too. Instead, the organizers were mixing an historical exhibition match with a serious sporting contest.

In this tournament, the games with Karpov were like a sideshow. But the sideshow put additional pressure on Anand, Kramnik and myself. Karpov could play without expectations but we three were expected to do well against him. Anand was the one who suffered from this. He was so shocked at losing to Karpov in round 2 that he could not beat me from a winning position in the next round. I think Karpov spoiled the performances of the other players in this event. I eagerly wanted to prove that the organizers were wrong to invite him to this tournament.

On each of the four days I was scheduled to play Karpov in the first game. Unfortunately, this was a disadvantage for me, as he was still fresh. Whoever played Karpov in the third and final round of each day had an easier time, for by then he was too tired to play well. This privilege fell to Kramnik. He scored plus two from it: When Karpov was White, the former world champion made quick draws, and when he was Black, he lost twice.

And so it was that Karpov and I played in the first round. After a tense struggle, the game ended in a draw. In the final position he stood better, but he only had around thirty seconds left on his clock to my minute. I suppose I could have tried to win on time, but if I was going to win I wanted to do it cleanly, so we agreed a draw. Then I drew with Kramnik, and in the last game of the day I beat Anand quite comfortably.

Anand switched to playing 1 d4 against me in the tournament, avoiding a theoretical discussion in the Najdorf variation. That was my tactic in the Microsoft game, too! However, away from his usual territory, he was less familiar with the opening than I was. I managed to gain the upper hand quite quickly and win our first encounter of the tournament.

30TH JUNE

DAY 2 OF FRANKFURT GIANTS

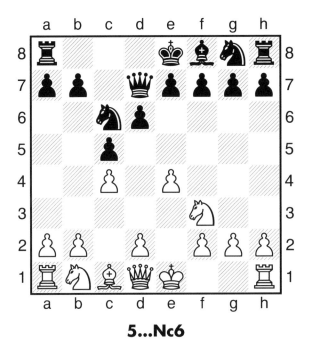

5...Nc6

Analysts' Recommendations: Krush, 5...Nc6; Paehtz, 5...Nc6; Felecan, 5...Nc6; Bacrot, no move submitted.

Voting Results: 5...Nc6, 5,560; 5...Nf6, 808; 5...e5, 328; 5...Qg4, 246; 5...g6, 211.

The World played the standard move, developing the queen's knight onto a good central square.

This was a dangerous day for me in Frankfurt. I miraculously escaped with a draw against Anand—at one point I was completely lost—and with Kramnik I was close to the edge, but I managed to hold on. Against Karpov I mishandled the opening, and after a tough struggle the game ended in a draw.

Karpov was excellent in fighting for survival, but there was no creativity in his play whatsoever. In our games, he constantly found himself in trouble—on the board and with the clock—but wriggled brilliantly. Nevertheless, his play was all about "escaping," nothing more.

It was a difficult day, but after I survived it, I knew that I would win the tournament.

1ST JULY

DAY 3 OF FRANKFURT GIANTS

(chess diagram)

6 Nc3

Returning to the Internet game, I had a slightly more difficult decision to make. Instead of 6 Nc3, I thought about playing **6 d4** cxd4 7 Nxd4 Nf6 8 Nc3. Then I would have to reckon with 8...Qg4, forcing an endgame. Indeed, this possibility was already under discussion on the Microsoft website. Even though the position is slightly worse for Black, I was reluctant to go in for it. First, with best play the position should be a draw. Second, and perhaps even more importantly, I was eager to keep the position as complex as possible, and that meant avoiding a queen exchange. In that case I felt there would be more chance of the World choosing the wrong path. Having discussed the situation with Yuri, I decided to stick with 6 Nc3.

I had 12 hours to make this decision, but that time disappears too quickly when playing in a tournament. Look at my hours: I received moves around 3:30 PM Central European Time, and I had till 3 AM to send my move. In the afternoon and evening I was playing in the Frankfurt tournament, so that meant I had just a few hours late in the evening to choose my move. For that reason it was important to postpone any major decisions about the World game until after July 12th.

I was now hoping to tempt my opponents into playing **6...e5**, locking the center. While this is not a terrible move, I think it would give White a small but enduring advantage: Black's bishop, blocked by its own pawns, is rather a poor piece, and I would have an easy plan of attacking on the queenside by advancing my pawn to b4. The World wisely decided against this course.

My wife, Yulia, arrived on this third day of the Frankfurt tournament. One of the first events she accompanied me to was the PCA speed tournament in Paris in 1995 where I beat Kramnik in a very tense final. She must be my lucky mascot, for this third day was when I really reached my stride. I played what was perhaps my best game of the event, and strangely enough, it was against Kramnik.

Before that, in the first game of the day, I had Black against Karpov. I had the better prospects throughout and he ran short of time, but defended stubbornly. Once again, in the final position I could have pressed to win on time, but by that stage my advantage was purely symbolic, so we agreed a draw.

Against Kramnik I didn't get any real advantage from the opening, but it was a tricky enough position, and I ended by crashing through to his king in the middle. In the final game of the day against Anand, I produced a new move early in the opening to which he could find nothing better than repeat the position, and so we agreed a draw. I had survived both his attempts to beat me with White, so realistically the danger from Anand was over.

The tournament had to be my first priority for the time being. The Microsoft game was not playing an important role in my life—I did not even set up the pieces on the chessboard. Sometimes I chatted about it with Yuri over coffee, but that was about it; it was just somewhere in the background.

2ND JULY

DAY 4 OF FRANKFURT

6...Nf6

Analysts' Recommendations: Krush, 6...g6; Paehtz, 6...Ne5; Felecan,
6...Nf6; Bacrot, 6...Nf6.

Voting Results: 6...Nf6, 3,405; 6...g6, 1,935; 6...Ne5, 355; 6...e5,
215; 6...Nd4, 169.

A normal move, developing the second knight into the center, but I had
half expected the World to play **6...g6**.

The day before I had bumped into Danny King, the event moderator, in
the hotel lobby (he was one of the live commentators at the speed
tournament). Danny said, "The World's going to follow your game with
Shirov!" I wasn't going to give anything away, but I couldn't help grinning.

If 6...g6, then after 7 d4 Black does not capture, but plays instead
7...Bg7, with the idea 8 d5 Bxc3+ 9 bxc3—as I had tried with Black against
Alexei Shirov in 1996. The opening turned out well for me on that
occasion, but, as I have since researched the position in great detail, I would
have relished going into this highly complex line again, even with White.

My task was simple: I was looking for positions that would be difficult for the analysts to explain to the World players. I guessed that communication was going to be their main problem. And no matter how good the advice, each analyst would be fighting against three others.

The last day at Frankfurt finished well for me. A win over Karpov, then two easy draws, brought me exactly to my target score—and first place by a margin of one and a half points in front of Anand and Kramnik, with Karpov in clear last place.

Mission accomplished.

3RD JULY

FRANKFURT

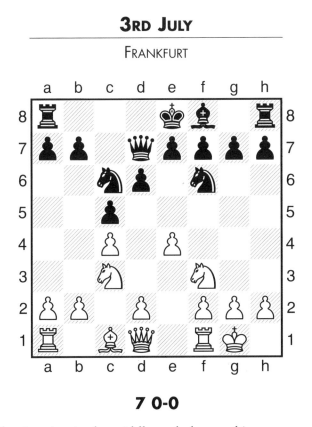

7 0-0

Before the situation in the middle explodes, my king evacuates.

Instead, I could have played **7 d4** straightaway, but there was still the possibility of 7...cxd4 8 Nxd4 Qg4 exchanging queens, as on the previous turn, so I decided against it.

4TH JULY

FRANKFURT TO MOSCOW

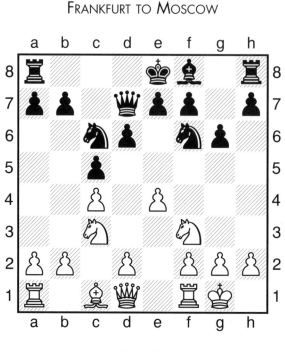

7...g6

Analysts' Recommendations: Krush 7...g6; Paehtz, 7...g6; Felecan, 7...g6; Bacrot, 7...Ne5

Voting Results: 7...g6, 3,086; 7...Ne5, 400; 7...e5, 332; 7...e6, 279; 7...0-0-0, 197.

The World prepares to fianchetto—the most usual method of development in this position.

It was interesting to see Bacrot recommending **7...Ne5**. It is rather a rare continuation, and perhaps not a bad move. Black attempts to take the tension out of the position by exchanging another pair of minor pieces. It took me some time on the plane back to Moscow to figure out how to deal with it—but that's for another day.

I returned home to Moscow with a feeling of great relief and satisfaction. This victory at Frankfurt concluded a winning streak for me in the first half of 1999. I had proved myself at every type of chess: I had won three classical chess tournaments, Wijk-aan-Zee, Linares and Sarajevo; the speed event in Frankfurt; and even the strong blitz tournament in Wijk-aan-Zee.

It felt like I was on holiday. The game was on the right track. I had finished all my serious chess for the first half of the year, and I was about to go to my summer training camp in Croatia. I have always enjoyed going there, working on my physical strength, studying chess, and relaxing. And, this time, I would be preparing for my world championship match against Vishy Anand.

5TH JULY

MOSCOW

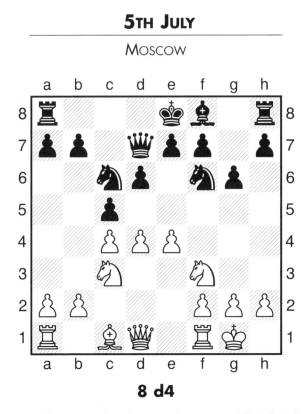

8 d4

I could wait no longer to break open the center. If I left it for another move, then the bishop comes to g7, indirectly controlling the d4 square, and so restraining my central pawn break. In that case I would have no advantage at all.

Back in Moscow I put my feet up for a few days. As I spend so much time travelling, it is vital for me to have a base where I can relax properly.

Garry with wife, Yulia, and son, Vadim

I grew up in Baku, the capital of the old Soviet Republic of Azerbaijan. My father, Kim, a Russian Jew, died when I was 6 years old. My mother, Klara, is Armenian. Although I lived happily in Baku for the first twenty-seven years of my life, in January 1990 I was forced, along with my family and many others, to flee my Heimat, following anti-Armenian *pogroms* by Azeri nationalists. The Armenian community, which made up a sizeable minority in the mainly Muslim city, simply does not exist anymore—many lost their lives and the rest had to flee. It goes without saying that my flight from Baku had a disruptive effect on my life. Even having relocated to Moscow, it took me years to settle into the right apartment, but now I have it. This really is home. Situated a quiet fifteen-minute walk from the Kremlin, it is really three apartments joined into one, and very functionally designed. Here I can enjoy family life with my wife, my son Vadim, and my mother. This is normality; this is stability.

If I wish I can always retreat to my study to keep in touch with the rest of the world, or work on chess—so long as my son doesn't run in to play on the computer with his usual cry of "Daddy, let's work!" His favorite trick is to operate the printer—he loves to see the paper spilling out.

But normally this is the perfect place to settle down and collect my thoughts.

6TH JULY

MOSCOW

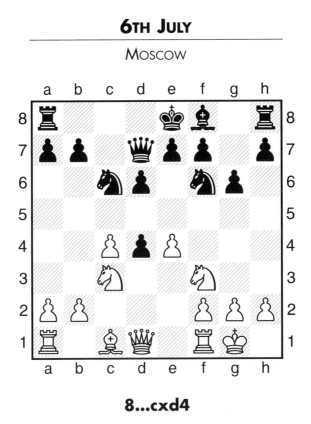

8...cxd4

Analysts' Recommendations: Krush, 8...cxd4; Paehtz, 8...cxd4; Felecan, 8...cxd4; Bacrot, 8...cxd4.

Voting Results: 8...cxd4, 5,358; 8...Nxd4, 265; 8...0-0-0, 139; 8...Bg7, 130; 8...e5, 75.

Black has to capture the pawn in the middle. Instead, if Black continues developing with **8...Bg7**, then 9 d5 attacks the knight, gaining space and time.

7TH JULY

MOSCOW

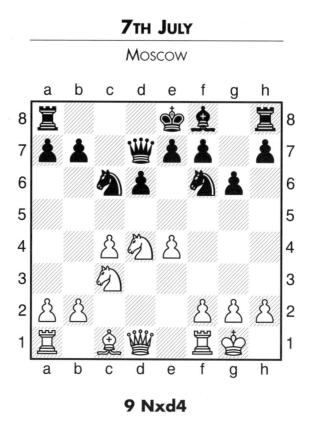

9 Nxd4

Naturally, I recaptured the pawn. With this last exchange I have constructed the so-called "Maroczy Bind" against Black's Sicilian pawn formation.

Born in 1870, Geza Maroczy from Hungary was one of the most successful players of the early 20th century. He employed this formation of pawns on e4 and c4 against the Sicilian to great effect, so much so that it was once thought to automatically give White a good game. Following Maroczy, Mikhail Botvinnik's famous victories in the 1930s seemingly put a curse on Black's position. White's aim is to control as much space as possible with the pawns in the center, preventing Black from breaking out from behind the first three rows. However, theoretical opinion has shifted since those days, and it has been proven that Black's counter chances are adequate.

From a historical perspective, one of the crucial games with this system was Portisch-Andersson from Milan in 1975. It had a revolutionary impact as it was one of the first occasions where a strong Grandmaster was unable to contain Black's counter play. Following Ulf Andersson's example, many others, including myself, experimented with the Black side of this system. It became known as the "Hedgehog"—anyone who rushed too hard at the modest structure would get a nasty stab!

Nevertheless, I was happy to play against the system as the strategy is complex. This suited my needs, and looking at the statistics of games with the Maroczy, the odds are actually still in White's favor.

8TH JULY

MOSCOW

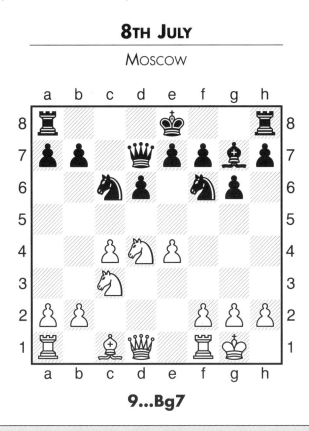

9...Bg7

Analysts' Recommendations: Krush, 9...Bg7; Paehtz, 9...Bg7; Felecan, 9...Bg7; Bacrot, 9...Bg7.

Voting Results: 9...Bg7, 5,206; 9...Nxd4, 452; 9...e5, 294; 9...0-0-0, 109; 9...Qg4, 64.

The bishop develops onto the longest diagonal, casting a shadow across the entire board. For the next two months this bishop was to be the bane of my life.

Black now threatens ...Nxe4, winning a pawn as the knight on d4 is *en prise*. I cannot defend the knight with **10 Be3** as 10...Ng4, threatening to win my important bishop for the knight, would then be awkward. Therefore, I have to move the knight on d4.

9TH JULY

MOSCOW TO PRAGUE

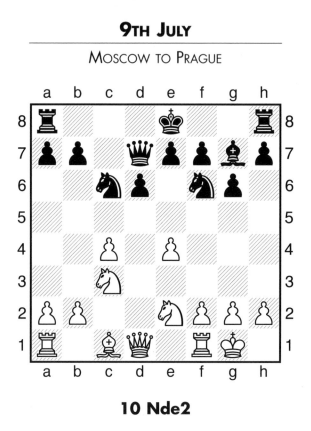

10 Nde2

The knight retreats but finds a new role. As the other knight on c3 is potentially in the line of fire of the bishop on g7, and later from a Black rook if it arrives on c8, then from e2 the knight performs a useful function by protecting its colleague.

So far, everything was going according to plan. The game was still following the path of past experience, so little thought had been required up to this moment. There was renewed interest in this variation following the Kramnik-Gelfand match in 1994 in which it was played twice. The first of those games now continued 10...0-0 11 f3 a6 12 a4 Rfc8 13 b3 Qd8 14 Kh1 Nd7 15 Bg5 Qa5 16 Qd2 Nc5 17 Rab1. White is attempting to squeeze Black into submission.

This was the rough model I had in mind when I went into the whole variation. I thought this position would give the World a variety of options to choose from and, with a bit of luck, lead to confusion within their ranks. My aim was to divide and conquer, the oldest ploy in the book. Added to that, I believed that with this kind of position it would be difficult for any expert to communicate to the public exactly what strategy to follow.

10 Nde2 was the last move I made from Moscow. I was sitting in my study having just sent it down the line when it suddenly struck me: "What about **Qe6**?"

I started going through variations in my head: "Okay, I play 11 Nd5, threatening the fork on c7, then if 11...Rc8, 12 f3—fine, my position is rock solid and they have just wasted time with the queen. And if they sacrifice the exchange . . . ? It's unclear. But they cannot play ...Qe6! Garry, what the hell are you thinking of? They will castle! Danny King keeps telling them every day, "Castle! Castle!"

It was a moment not of fear, but of apprehension. Then I reasoned, "Fine, if it happens, I will figure it out."

I went to Prague on July 9 to open the Shirov-Polgar match and to commentate on the first game. Besides being the current holder of the Eurotel Trophy, I did this as a favor to the organizer Bessel Kok.

In the mid 1980s, Bessel was the president of Swift, a pioneering electronic banking company based in Brussels. He had a passion for chess, which he demonstrated through his support of a whole series of tournaments. He entered the chess world with a mission: Top events had to be transformed into something more professional, both for players and spectators. And in the events he organized, he succeeded in doing so brilliantly.

In 1986, we combined to create the Grandmasters Association (GMA), for a time perhaps the most successful chess enterprise there has been. As well as running a whole series of excellent tournaments, we came very close to wresting the world of chess from the hands of the FIDE bureaucrats, but there was a split in our views on the way the GMA should proceed. We failed in our aim, and the organization collapsed. Then Bessel moved to Prague, becoming president of Czech Telecom, and played no further role in the development of chess. Our paths didn't cross for some time.

Then he reappeared, organizing a few small chess events, before coming up with the idea of the EuroTel Trophy. This is an annual six-game challenge match between two leading players for a healthy prize fund of $100,000. I played the first match for the trophy in 1998 with Jan Timman. As usual with Bessel's events, it was superbly organized.

I was invited to defend my title in 1999, this time against Judit Polgar, but as I did not want to have any more matches prior to the world championship, I declined. Instead, I recommended to Bessel that he invite Alexei Shirov in my place, as compensation for our match falling through last year. Shirov vs. Polgar would guarantee an attractive event; and Alexei would make some good money. I was glad he was able to play.

It seems that no good deed goes unpunished. It was said that my motive for recommending Shirov was to assuage my guilt for the cancellation of our match in 1998. This was nonsense. If I had been responsible for the match falling through, then that might have been true, but that was the sponsor's decision. I suffered from its failure, too.

Even though I wasn't playing this year, I was pleased to attend the event in support of Bessel. Prague 1998 had refreshed my good memories of the GMA tournaments of the late 1980s. It was also the first board meeting of Club Kasparov—now Kasparov Chess Online; and besides that, Bessel was assisting with the organization of my world championship match with Anand.

Bessel has a glamorous touch. For the opening ceremony he had invited Woody Harrelson, the star of *Natural Born Killers*, who happened to be in the Czech Republic visiting a film festival. He is a big chess fan. We played a short exhibition game at the opening ceremony, and it is clear that he has more than natural born ability—particularly when assisted by Grandmasters Seirawan and Sosonko, who were commentators at the event.

Bessel likes to show that chess attracts people of quality from all kinds of backgrounds: film stars, bankers, politicians, CEOs of major corporations, and so on. I fully support him in his efforts to raise the prestige of the game. Bessel and I have always been united in the belief that chess deserves better than its current lot.

10TH JULY

PRAGUE

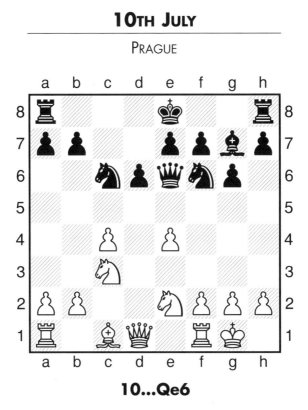

10...Qe6

Analysts' Recommendations: Krush 10...Qe6; Paehtz 10...Qe6; Felecan 10...0-0; Bacrot 10...0-0.

Voting Results: 10...Qe6, 2,959; 10...0-0, 2,062; 10...0-0-0, 78; 10...Qg4, 66; 10...e5, 64.

If **10...Qe6** hadn't been played, it would have been an interesting game, but nothing compared to what we witnessed in the next hundred days. Apparently against all classical principles, the queen moves into a jungle of pieces without fear for its own safety.

Normally, it is extremely risky to move the queen out at such an early stage of the game. The queen is the most valuable piece on the board, so every time it gets attacked by another piece, it will just have to move away. It is more usual for the queen to enter the game once a safe square becomes available, usually following piece exchanges. Added to that, in this position Black's king remains in the center of the board, providing another target for White to aim at.

So why was it played? After 10...Qe6, Black threatens to capture two pawns, the one on c4 with the queen and the one on e4 with the knight. I can hold both pawns, but only at the cost of playing some of my pieces to awkward squares. In fact, a later game played in December 1999 at the European Team Championships confirmed this assessment—it seems that one of the players, at least, had been following the Microsoft game!

Damljanovic—Stohl, Batumi 1999, continued:

11 Qb3 (defending the c-pawn and, indirectly, the e-pawn, through the attack on b7. The problem is that the pawn on c4 needs to be protected by a pawn if it is to be really secure, so White has to lose time later on for some regrouping) 11...0–0 12 Nf4 Qc8 13 Nfd5 e6 14 Nxf6+ Bxf6 15 Bh6 Rd8 16 Rac1 Ne5 17 Ne2 Qc6 18 Qc2 Rac8 19 b3 d5. White managed to save the e and c pawns, but Black has exploited the poor position of his opponent's pieces to seize the initiative. Black went on to win in 35 moves.

To avoid such a fate, the only thing left for me was to plunge into unfathomable complications with **11 Nd5**.

I sent a message of congratulations to the World Team via Microsoft on their new move 10...Qe6—they deserved it. I had already made a few humorous comments when sending my moves—which Microsoft was keen for me to do in our original discussions—but then I decided that enough was enough. I changed my attitude. It didn't matter if these comments were light-hearted, I no longer wanted to betray anything about my mood. For me, the game was getting more serious.

11TH JULY

PRAGUE

11 Nd5

Threatening a knight fork on c7. Black can of course prevent it, but that would not be the best course. For instance, **11...Rc8** prevents the knight check but would leave Black in a poor position after the simple move 12 f3, defending the e-pawn. Then the queen would be left looking silly on e6, biting on White's solid pawn chain. Soon it would be attacked and forced to retreat, having gained precisely nothing.

Of course, the knight on d5 cannot be taken, as White recaptures with the pawn, setting up another fork. No, there is only one decent possibility for Black, **11...Qxe4**, grabbing a pawn in the middle, even though it allows that check on c7. There is simply no turning back. Of course, this was all planned before 10...Qe6 was played.

After I played Nd5 and saw that all the analysts recommended 11...Qxe4, I was worried. I realized that the game was going to be wildly complicated—not just for my opponents, but for me, too.

I sat down in my hotel room in Prague to study the position on my own. I looked at the World's latest recommendations, and I read Irina

Krush's commentary—it was long and detailed. I couldn't help thinking, "Did she really do all this alone?" There were about a dozen pages of analysis, and she was quoting suggestions from many different players. That was serious. Irina gave two types of commentaries: one that was for chess novices; and one that contained highly sophisticated analysis. From that I had the feeling that her commentaries were compiled, that there were different people working with different roles, and that sent danger signals to me. While Irina's commentary (really the Smart Chess commentary—her management team) was lengthy, the other three analysts were producing nothing to match it, just a few brief lines to back up their recommendations, much as we had originally envisaged their roles would be. This was partly to do with language difficulties, but perhaps mainly because they did not have the same management support. Whatever the reason, the effect was that Irina's profile on the site grew, and her analysis was followed by the vast majority of voters.

Back to the position. I considered the variation **11...Qxe4** 12 Nc7+ Kd7 13 Nxa8 Qxc4 14 Nc3 Rxa8 15 Re1. I studied the position for about twenty minutes, and naturally I tried to play 15...Kc7, to bring the king over to safety on the queenside, but then I have 16 h3 Rc8 17 Be3 Kb8 18 Rc1, and White is better because Black's king is still a bit exposed. The material balance of a knight and two pawns against a rook is potentially favorable for Black, but it is difficult to restore coordination, so White has the better position.

The next day I had a brief discussion of these variations with Yasser Seirawan—after all, it was quite an interesting position; but our chat wasn't at all serious. I repeat, at this time it still didn't feel like a serious game. Yasser has not been a noted supporter of mine in the last few years, but somehow the splendid atmosphere of the event reminded us both of the glory days of the GMA, putting us in a good mood.

That was my state of mind as I left Prague: I was a little disconcerted at what seemed to be this team lining up to battle against me, but I still wasn't concerned about the position. And I was about to start my summer break. There is hardly a better feeling.

12TH JULY

ARRIVED IN CROATIA

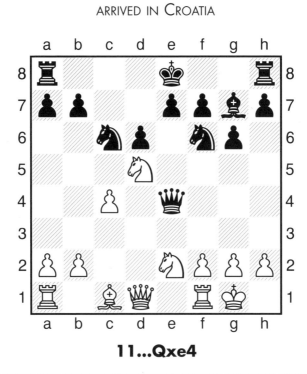

11...Qxe4

Analysts' Recommendations: Krush 11...Qxe4; Paehtz 11...Qxe4; Felecan, no recommendation; Bacrot 11...Qxe4.

Voting Results: 11...Qxe4, 4,022; 11...O-O, 371; 11...Rc8, 309; 11...Qd7, 228; 11...0-0-0, 206.

The next few moves were completely forced for both sides. To justify 10...Qe6 Black has to capture the pawn in the middle, even though it allows the knight fork on c7.

It was great to arrive in Croatia. For the third year I was staying in a huge house, just forty yards from the sea on the outskirts of a holiday town called Makarska. With thirteen bedrooms, it's almost like a small hotel. Each year we are there for around forty-five to fifty days, so by now I really feel at home.

There was a big party of us there: my mother, my wife, my then 3-year-old son, Vadim—born on October 28th 1996; Yuri Dokhoian, joined by his wife for the first few weeks; Alexander Shakarov, my old friend and coach from my childhood in Baku, who now looks after my library and computers; a doctor who is a family friend; some of my cousins; then there were other friends coming in and out, staying for a few days at a time; and for the last three days there was a French film crew working on a documentary about me (due for its premiere in Paris in September 2000). A Croatian family was living there permanently, working as housekeepers.

In some people's minds, "Croatia" evokes negative associations, but I have been visiting the western part since 1993 and I love it. These summer vacations have helped to bring stability into my life.

For ten years, from 1980 until 1989, I used to go to a training camp on the shores of the Caspian Sea, just outside Baku. That was a very important part of my preparation. It helped to replenish my energy. But after my family's flight from the *pogroms* in Baku in 1990, we were forced to look elsewhere for a summer location. We tried Spain, then Los Angeles, then in 1992 Spain again, but somehow they never felt quite right.

Since 1993 we have found the right place. It reminds me a little of my old training camp near Baku. The Adriatic is beautiful, perhaps one of the cleanest seas in Europe. Ironically, the tragedy of the war has helped the ecology of the region enormously: industry ground to a halt at that time, so the sea became cleaner. Croatia is also much closer to Russia than the other locations we tried—we understand the language and, at first at least, a visa was not required.

For four summers we stayed further north in Istria, near Italy. Then in 1996 when the war was completely over, we decided to move south to somewhere along the Split-Dubrovnik coastline. My mother did some scouting with some Croatian friends, and they found a great place. Now that we are all happy here we will keep coming back, and that's just how I like it. Knowing where I will be in the summer of 2000 is a comforting feeling. There is enough chaos in my life, so it is nice to be able to look forward to something with certainty, knowing that I will not have to expend energy adapting to new conditions.

Although I had enjoyed playing in tournaments all over the former Yugoslavia, in 1992, after the Balkan war had broken out, I decided to nail my colors to the mast. After the *pogroms* in Baku, I formed a simple belief.

The criminals and killers have no nationality or religion. They are simply wrong. I believe that from the very beginning the Serbs were the prime aggressors in the whole area, and that is why I decided to support Bosnia and Croatia in whatever way I could.

It was under my instigation and pressure that a vote took place at the 1992 European team championships in Debrecen, which led to the expulsion of the Serbian team. I was not alone in my views: the vote was carried by 28-2.

I made a tour of almost all the major Croatian cities, giving simultaneous chess exhibitions in aid of children. I played in the Krajina area after the liberation from the Serbs. I even went to Sarajevo during the siege in 1994 to play in a charity exhibition in the headquarters of the French battalion. Because the airport was closed, I had to leave in a Russian armored car, through minefields, travel over Mount Igman to Mostar, and then fly by Croatian military helicopter to Split.

That is why I am a welcome guest in this region. I like the place and I like the people. When I played in Sarajevo in 1999, people would come up to me on the streets thanking me for visiting—they remembered I was also there five years before when conditions were not as comfortable. I get the same reaction in Makarska. People recognize me and like me, but at the same time they respect my privacy as they know I am there to work and to relax with my family.

In former times, Yugoslavia was a fanatical chess country. There were strong players wherever one went, and the average standard was probably higher than in the USSR. In spite of the war, the chess tradition is still very much alive, and it is pleasant to live in an environment where one is respected and appreciated.

In Makarska my usual regime was to take a light breakfast, followed by a great deal of physical exercise: rowing, swimming, and gym work. Then I would sleep for an hour—(by then, I would have to). I would take lunch around 3 PM, and from 4 PM till 9.30 PM serious chess study. That is the best time for me to work. The primary objective for our work in the afternoon—at least at the beginning of my stay—was preparing for my world championship match with Vishy Anand. Then I would have dinner and afterward go for a walk with my wife and my son.

However, the day wasn't quite over for me. This summer I was providing coverage of the FIDE knockout tournament in Las Vegas for the Kasparov

ChessOnline website. I wrote seven reports in total, one at the end of each round. That would take from approximately 11:30 PM till 2 AM.

I am not giving away any secrets when I say I am not a fan of FIDE, yet I cannot deny that their knockout tournament was one of the most important chess events of 1999. When you get so many strong players competing for good prize money, the competitive atmosphere is bound to produce interesting chess, so it was important for me to cover the tournament, not just for the website and the rest of the chess world, but for my own benefit, too.

And, last but not least in my daily schedule, starting around July 19th when the game position became more tense, from 11 PM until midnight and later, we would analyze the Microsoft game. That was the time for Boris Alterman in Tel Aviv to get involved, working with us on the other end of a phone line.

13TH JULY

CROATIA

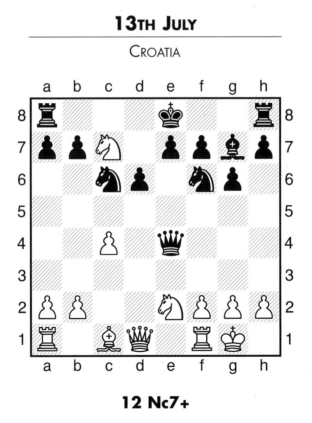

12 Nc7+

As my pawn center is crumbling I had to go for the rook in the corner.

14TH JULY

CROATIA

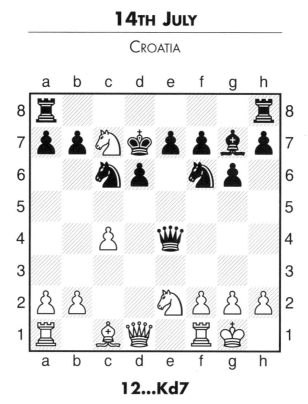

12...Kd7

Analysts' Recommendations: Krush 12...Kd7; Paehtz 12...Kd7; Felecan, no recommendation; Bacrot 12...Kd7.

Voting Results: 12...Kd7, 6,567; 12...Kd8, 304; 12...Kf8, 58; 12...0-0, 46; 12...0-0-0, 26.

The king must move to d7 so that after White captures on a8, the other rook can swing over to take the knight.

It was around this time that I got my first telephone call from Boris Alterman in Israel. It was a wake up call in many ways.

Boris asked: "Garry Kimovich, are you following Khalifman's analysis?"

"Khalifman?"

"Khalifman and the players at his GM School in St. Petersburg. You know how much analysis is being done there? Everybody is analyzing the game. Garry, you are up against a really powerful force. You had better take it seriously."

I had not been looking at the website in great detail so I simply hadn't appreciated the number of people on the World Team working against me, and in the case of Khalifman and his friends in St. Petersburg, the quality and depth of the analysis. Anyway, although the game hadn't gone exactly as I had wanted it to, I didn't sense any real danger.

"Okay Boris, what's the problem? I play 14 Nc3, and Re1..."

"Garry, 15...Rd8 and then ....Ke8."

In Prague, in the variation **13 Nxa8** Qxc4 14 Nc3 Rxa8 15 Re1, I had only looked at the Black king running toward the queenside with 15...Kc7, followed by ...Rc8 and ...Kb8; but, even though it is more time consuming, Boris was right, the king is far safer hiding on the other side, the kingside, behind the cover of 5 pawns, not two. 15...Rd8! is the correct move, preparing to drop the king back to e8 with the rook covering the d6 pawn.

I assembled Yuri and Alexander Shakarov into the room, explained the situation to them, and we began to analyze the position on the board. I tried 16 a4 Ke8 17 a5. It looked interesting. I called Boris back.

"Garry," he said, "You are not taking this seriously. Black plays 17...d5 18 Ra4 Qc5: They have two pawns in the center, the black king is well protected. You have to be worse."

I was looking at the position without a computer, and my instinct told me that White's initiative would be difficult to control. In a practical, classical game I believe this would be the correct assessment: With limited time at our disposal, we humans often find it difficult to take a cold-blooded view when under pressure; one might overcompensate, for instance, and play too defensively. However, this was a very different type of encounter. Using a fearless computer, Boris realized that with precise defense, White's activity would eventually come to nothing.

Still, I just didn't want to believe that I could be sitting in a worse position. I looked at the position again. The chess half of my brain could understand the problems on the board, but the other half just didn't want to take the game with the seriousness that it demanded. It took some persuasion from Yuri and Boris before I reluctantly accepted their view. In the longterm, with those two center pawns, Black could dominate the position.

What a way to start the summer.

15TH JULY

CROATIA

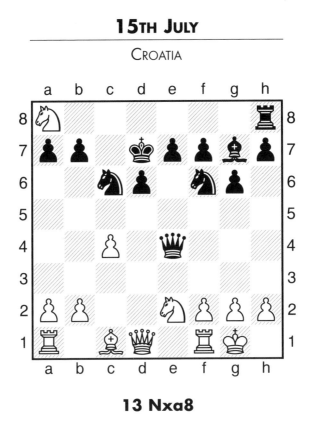

13 Nxa8

I had no choice. I was glad to take the rook in the corner, but not quite so pleased that my center was disappearing. If Black recaptures the knight straightaway, then he would only have a pawn and knight for the rook—a poor trade. But as the white knight cannot escape from the corner, Black swipes off another pawn before capturing it. . .

"Garry, you are up against a really powerful force. You had better take it seriously."

—*Boris Alteman, July 13, 1999*

16TH JULY

CROATIA

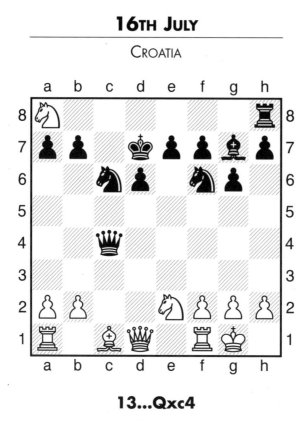

13...Qxc4

Analysts' Recommendations: Krush 13...Qxc4 Paehtz 13...Qxc4; Felecan 13...Qxc4; Bacrot 13...Qxc4.

Voting Results: 13..Qxc4, 6,157; 13...Rxa8, 388; 13...Ng4, 61; 13...Nb4, 28; 13...Nh5, 15.

Black collects a second pawn before turning to deal with the knight. It cannot escape from the corner.

"Controlling the center should be one of the primary objectives at the start of the game."

—Garry Kasparov

17TH JULY

CROATIA

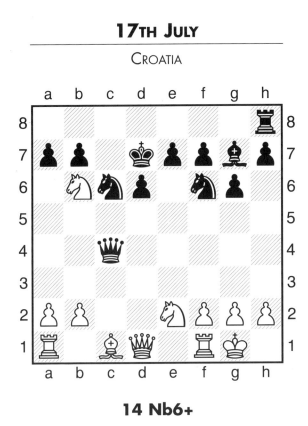

14 Nb6+

By this time it was clear to me that I had to play Nb6+. If instead **14 Nc3**, as I had previously examined, Black would have the better position with absolutely no risk. The problem is that there would be no real weaknesses for me to target. In that case the best thing I could hope for would be a dubious endgame, with perhaps a few drawing chances.

Therefore, I played the kamikaze sacrifice 14 Nb6+. The knight cannot be saved, so it might as well create as much damage in its departure as possible. In this way I give Black doubled pawns and so create a tiny chink in my opponent's armor. But, I have to admit, I didn't know what to do next.

18TH JULY

CROATIA

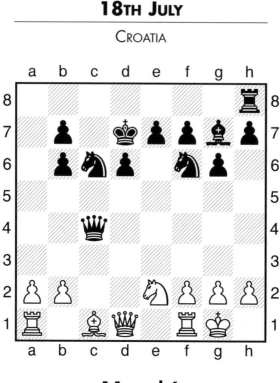

14...axb6

Analysts' Recommendations: Krush, 14...axb6; Paehtz, 14...axb6; Felecan, 14...axb6; Bacrot, 14...axb6.

Voting Results: 14...axb6, 5,162; 14...Kc7, 37; 14...Ke6, 19; 14...Ke8, 8; 14...Kd8, 4.

Naturally, Black captures. The pawns on the queenside are now doubled, a slight but potentially significant weakness as they can no longer protect each other. At least that was my hope. I needed a target to attack in Black's position, and I couldn't find one.

This is the first time that the position had stabilized since 10...Qe6, so I took stock. First, the balance of pieces: In the flurry of captures over the last few moves, Black gained a knight and two pawns, and I took the rook in the corner. Going by standard chess values, that is a roughly equal material balance.

Then I appraised the strengths and weaknesses of the White and Black positions. The most obvious difference between the two sides is the positioning of the kings. Mine is tucked away in the corner behind a barrier of pawns, totally safe; Black's, on the other hand, is still in the middle of the board. Normally this would not be a good spot for the Black king— castling is standard practice in top games—but here Black can get away with it as the king also has a shield of pawns for protection. In fact, it is these pawns which give Black, potentially, an excellent position.

Controlling the center should be one of the primary objectives at the start of the game, and the best way to do that is with the pawns. Imagine if those two central pawns on the d and e files were to roll down the board: They would be tremendously powerful as I have no pawns to oppose them. At the moment such a plan is simply impossible. Black's king would be too exposed. However, if the queens were exchanged, reducing my atttacking chances, then the pawn advance would become a possibility.

Aside from the pawns, what about the positioning of the other pieces? Black is actually better developed than White. In particular that bishop on g7, searing across the long diagonal, has great potential; for the moment it is far better than its counterpart on c1. All in all it was a highly unclear position, but I did not think that one could talk in terms of White having any advantage at all.

The sequence of moves since 10...Qe6 was practically forced, but then I was presented with a very difficult choice. Because of Black's active pieces, I could not develop my queenside very easily. At first I looked at **15 Nc3**, but I did not like the reply 15...b5—Black could equalize easily. The best I could hope for would be a draw.

Instead of 15 Nc3, I looked at **15 a4** to prevent Black playing ...b5. However, this has certain drawbacks: It weakens the b4 and b3 squares since they can no longer be covered by pawns. It is terribly complex, but I found more than one satisfactory reply for Black, for example, 15...Ne4, 15...Nd5, and even 15...Qd5.

19TH JULY

CROATIA

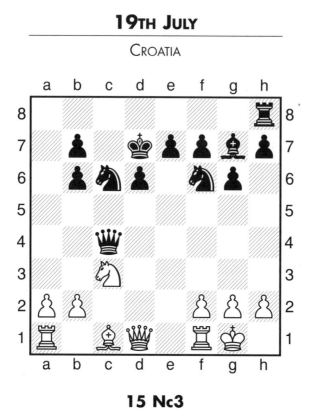

15 Nc3

Having racked my brains for days I finally decided on Nc3. Why? Because I realized that my goal in this position should be just to make a draw. Starting from Nb6+, I had a very simple agenda: to avoid losing.

At that point, having realized the danger, I had to be realistic. The opposition was not going to blunder, they were putting me under severe pressure, and they were dictating the terms of the game. Looking at their analysis and how comprehensively they studied the different paths in the position, it was clear that they were way ahead of me in their understanding of the position. Somehow, I had to catch up.

We formulated a battle plan. First, we had to gather all the information available on the web. Every day Boris would download the latest analysis from the Smart Chess team, as well as anything else that seemed useful from the Gaming Zone bulletin boards and other sites. Then we could sift through the information and see what direction their analysis was heading.

Many people on the bulletin boards said during the game that I had an unfair advantage because I could see the World's analysis. That was absolutely correct. That gave me an advantage—I wouldn't describe it as unfair though; it balanced the struggle. There were three of us with three computers versus thousands of them with hundreds of computers, so just the amount of positions they could analyze was immense. There was a chance that I could suddenly find myself in dire difficulties and it would simply be too late. There would be no blunder, no favor returned. From this moment on I realized we would have to work day and night to avoid defeat.

As I mentioned before, the move I feared in this position was **15...b5**, making a virtue of the doubled b-pawn to disrupt my position. It was recommended by the GM school in St. Petersburg and backed up with reams of analysis. We searched long and hard for a satisfactory answer but didn't really find one. I was concerned that my knight would be dislodged from c3, and I would lose all control over the central squares. A disaster. It demonstrates that "central control" is not an empty phrase in chess. It constitutes a serious advantage.

It is possible that at the time we overestimated Black's chances, but perhaps that was indicative of my state of mind. Now, six months later, in the middle of a Moscow winter, I can look at the position with a cooler, calmer head. In fact, White is able to generate sufficient counter chances.

If you are interested in a detailed analysis of the possibilities after 15...b5, I would direct you to the Kasparov ChessOnline website. Let me just give you one variation here: 15...b5 16 Be3 Rd8 17 Re1 Ng4 18 Re1 Nxe3 19 Rxe3 Bxc3 (otherwise the Knight will discrupt's Black's setup) 20 b3 Qd4 21 Rd3! As usual, White should avoid the ending. Black's queen moves away, White recaptures on c3, and the position is very unclear. White can use the rook on the third rank to attack weaknesses, but Black's pawn structure is fundamentally sound.

20TH JULY

CROATIA

15...Ra8

Analysts' Recommendations: Krush, 15...Ra8; Paehtz, 15...b5; Felecan, 15...d5; Bacrot, 15...Rd8.

Voting Results: 15...Ra8, 3,456; 15...b5, 1,056; 15...Rd8, 789; 15...d5, 354; 15...Ne4, 303.

I was glad to see that the four analysts each came up with a different recommendation, so there was a chance that in this complex position the voters could make the wrong choice. Indeed, it turned out that the move I had feared, 15...b5, was not played—and I breathed a big sigh of relief. However, I was faced instead with the aggressive 15...Ra8, originally a casual suggestion of the English Grandmaster Jonathan Speelman, and taken up and analyzed by the Krush contingent. If you look at the vote in this highly unclear position, it is clear that Irina Krush and Smart Chess were beginning to dominate the World Team.

15...Ra8 is a logical move: On h8 the rook was inactive, but now it swings to the semi-open file, putting pressure on the pawn on a2. Given the chance, the rook could also make an appearance on the fifth rank, swinging across to attack my kingside or threaten my queen.

At the time, after 15...Ra8 I felt I had no choice; it seemed to me that **16 a4** had to be played to block out the rook. If instead **16 Re1**, then Black seizes the initiative with 16...Ra5, bringing the rook into play along the fifth rank: 17 a4 Rf5! is worrying for White. (Incidentally, this reminds me of the twenty-third game from my 1986 world championship match against Karpov where I performed a similar maneuver with my rook).

However, I could have tried 16 Be3, which would transpose to variations after 15...b5 on the last move.

21ST JULY

CROATIA

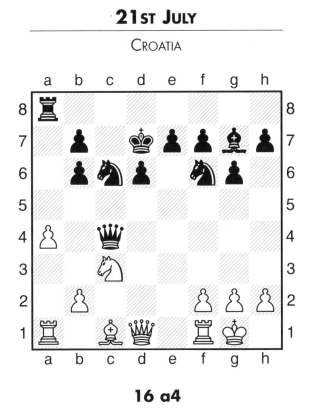

16 a4

I played a4 to neutralize the effectiveness of the rook on a8, but also to fix the pawn on b6. Now, for instance, moving the bishop to e3 to attack the b-pawn comes into consideration as it can no longer advance to b5.

If Black attempts to bring the rook into the game with **16...Ra5**, I would have blocked it out with 17 Nb5. Then I could attack the rook with Bd2 or go for the b-pawn with Be3. I wouldn't have any difficulties there, although Black is also fine. The World's reply was more dramatic and more dangerous.

Starting from 15...Ra8, I noticed a pattern in the play of Irina and her team: If there was a choice, they consistently went for the most aggressive and unexpected option. It seemed they were always attempting to whip up complications rather than play a line that resolved the situation. For instance, 15...Ra8 was played instead of 15...b5; then later on, 16...Ne4; 18...f5; and 19...Qb4 instead of 19...Qd4. There was hardly a moment for me to catch my breath. Even in classical chess, very few have been able to master this kind of strategy as it not only puts pressure on the opponent, but on the one creating the complications as well. Of past players, Fischer and Tal had this facility and, today, perhaps Shirov and I are the only ones similarly capable.

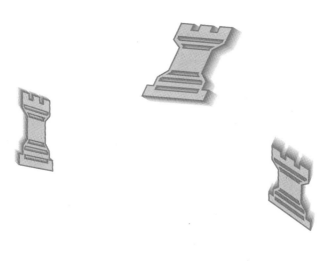

22ND JULY

CROATIA

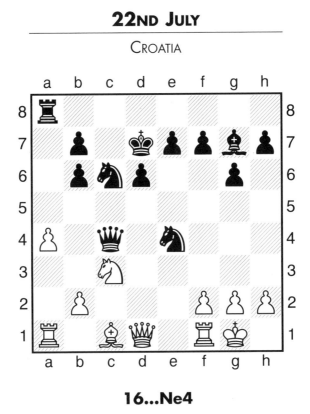

16...Ne4

> **Analysts' Recommendations:** Krush, 16...Ne4; Paehtz, 16...Ra5; Felecan, 16...Nd4; Bacrot, 16...d5.
>
> **Voting Results:** 16...Ne4, 3,482; 16...Nd4, 973; 16...Ra5, 886; 16...d5, 561; 16...Ng4, 165.

Offering the exchange of knights is a fundamentally sound decision. In the short-term, if Black plays carelessly, I have attacking chances; but in the long-term, with the powerful central pawn mass, Black has the better prospects. With every exchange, the pawn mass becomes more potent, and White's attacking prospects are reduced. In particular, an exchange of queens would be highly desirable for Black. That would instantly minimize the (potential) danger to Black's king; indeed the king would be well placed to support the center pawns. An exchange of knights brings Black a step closer to the long-term goal of an endgame.

This was a good move on the part of Black. Apart from anything else, it was going to be easier for the analysts to explain to the World Team what was happening as the position was opening and Black has greater room to maneuver.

Instead, Bacrot recommended **16...d5**. Claiming ground in the center would, on paper at least, have been a reasonable idea. However, for this kind of game, I think it would have been too dangerous. It would have been too difficult to convey the complex strategy to the voters. While the king is still in the middle, it is risky to begin pushing the center pawns, particularly while there are so many pieces on the board. One inaccurate move could have disastrous consequences for Black.

Though a pair of minor pieces was about to be exchanged, the tension increased with 16...Ne4. I had already anticipated it, but still, when the move appeared, I just thought, "My God, what is going on? This is getting out of control, it is so complicated."

When serious chess players get involved in a game, they become tense. I am no exception. A normal game lasts an average of four hours; and a normal tournament something like two weeks—quite stressful enough. But this game simply did not go away; for over one hundred days it was with me. It was like having to analyze and live through forty adjournments in match or tournament play.

Everybody in the house was concerned that I was expending too much energy, not just on the analysis, but simply brooding about the game itself. It was hanging over me the whole time, day and night. I would go to the beach, I would be rowing or eating, and I was still thinking about the position. It had become a competitive game that consumed me, and everybody knew it.

> *"My God, what is going on? This is getting out of control, it is so complicated."*
>
> *—Garry Kasparov, July 22*

Far from the usual relaxed atmosphere, the house in Croatia was like a war-time operations headquarters. Apart from the joint analysis sessions, Boris would call on the telephone from Israel with analysis; and Yuri would work on his own when I was writing my Las Vegas reports late into the night. Everybody became involved. My family and friends knew I was in danger.

Around this time, for me, the game became very personal and very serious. I already had my suspicions about the Smart Chess team representing Irina Krush, as they have connections with my old rival Anatoly Karpov, but now I saw that they were bending the rules to get Irina's recommendations voted in.

Instead of originally presenting 16...Ne4 as a move that would give Black good compensation for a pawn—which is true—she carefully avoided mentioning that it would involve giving up material. I suspect that she and her team were concerned that a pawn sacrifice would scare off the more cautious voter. In her analysis, she gave a false line claiming that Black was winning (see 18 Qb3). I am convinced that the Smart Chess team knew that White had a resource that would give me the better chances (even though it still should be a draw). The World Team players went along with it.

I also didn't like the way Irina used the names of strong players to support her move recommendations; Speelman and Khalifman, for instance. She used their chess-playing reputations to win people over to her side, when it should have just been her, with her own name, recommending a move. I felt this was going against the principles of the game. I spoke to Microsoft about it, but it was too late. The problem was that there were no clear rules set out before the game started, which is why, in the end, I didn't create a big fuss over the issue. The conduct of Irina and Smart Chess might have been against the spirit of what we had originally envisaged, but they were not breaking any rules.

I found myself in a frustrating situation. This game that had started out as an interesting experiment and which I hoped would be fun, had turned into a serious struggle: I was truly playing against the Rest of the World.

Just to add to my discomfort, I was being criticized in the Russian press. There were one or two articles comparing "Kasparov v. the World" with old games between Grandmasters and newspaper readers. For instance, Mikhail Tal played against the readers of *Trud*. Readers would send in moves and the games would last around six months. The quality of the games was mixed, to put it mildly. These journalists considered the Microsoft game to be the same as these traditional games from twenty-five years ago—according to them, the whole thing was just a joke, another desperate attempt to boost my own popularity in my fight with FIDE. The idea that it was a revolutionary technological breakthrough simply did not occur to them. Meanwhile, it felt like I was running for cover, spending hours and hours trying to find a good move. The newspapers just didn't understand what was going on.

I was getting riled, but I had to accept my fate. One day at lunch when I was complaining again, my mother told me, "Garry, you are playing the World. So what did you want, an easy ride? It was your decision to play this game. It's your cake—now eat it. It's okay. No complaints. Just do it."

Garry and his mother, Klara

"Garry, you are playing the World. So what did you want, an easy ride?. . . No complaints. Just do it."

—*Klara Kasparova*

23RD JULY

CROATIA

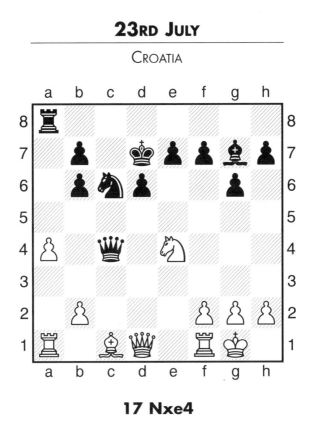

17 Nxe4

I had to acquiesce to the exchange of knights.

Instead, if **17 Nd5**, then Black has 17...Bd4! protecting the b-pawn and threatening to capture the knight on d5 with the queen; combined with the knight on e4 there is also dangerous pressure on f2. Or **17 Qd5** Qxd5 18 Nxd5 Ra6. The endgames are always good for Black because of the center pawns supported by the centralized king, and active minor pieces.

24TH JULY

CROATIA

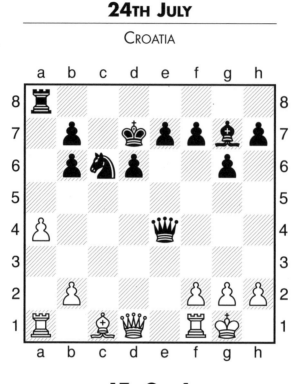

17...Qxe4

Analysts' Recommendations: Krush, 17...Qxe4; Paehtz, 17...Qxe4; Felecan, 17...Qxe4; Bacrot, 17...Qxe4.

Voting Results: 17...Qxe4, 5,824; 17...Ke6, 42; 17...Nd4, 26; 17...f5, 21; 17...Qxf1+, 16.

With the diagonal of the bishop on g7 now open, it is difficult for me to develop my bishop as the pawn on b2 is vulnerable.

I could push Black's queen away with **18 Re1**, but it would not help me a great deal. After 18...Qd4, with the positional "threat" of a queen exchange, Black is doing fine. If then 19 Qb3, Black has a better version of the game as Black's b-pawn is protected. For instance, the continuation 19...e6 20 Be3 Qxb2 21 Qxb2 Bxb2 22 Rab1 Bc3 24 Rec1 Ba5 25 Bxb6 Bxb6 26 Rxb6 Kc7 gives Black a very pleasant endgame.

25TH JULY

CROATIA

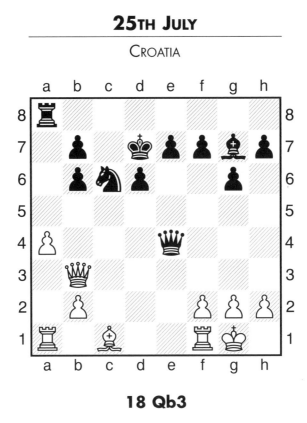

18 Qb3

To present Black with the most problems I felt I had to try this queen sortie, no matter how risky it was. Because of the forced captures beforehand, it meant we were lucky enough to have time to analyze the position in some detail after 18 Qb3—which was absolutely necessary. This was an important crossroads in the game.

First we had to reckon with the forcing move **18...Nd4**. White cannot play 19 Qxb6 as the queen would be lost: 19...Ra6 20 Qb4 Ne2+. Therefore 19 Qxf7 is forced. Now after 19... Nc2, White has the crafty move 20 Bd2! (any decent computer would find this move, that is why it is hard to believe that Irina and Co. did not also see it when they originally analyzed 16...Ne4. Instead, she gave here 20 Rb1 Ne1! winning for Black) 20...Nxa1 21 Re1 Qh4 (to protect e7) 22 Qd5 (threatening Qxb7+, winning the rook) 22...Rf8 (threatening ...Qxf2+) 23 Qxb7+ Ke8.

Now White has quite a choice of continuations. Apart from forcing an immediate draw by perpetual check, there are a couple of ways I could play for the win, though none of them is particularly convincing. For example,

24 g3 Qf6 25 Qc6+ (25 Qxb6 Nb3 holds the draw) 25...Kf7 26 Bc3 Qg5 27 Qxb6 Bxc3 28 bxc3 Qd2 29 Rxa1 Qxc3 30 Rb1. Although White is pressing, with best play the position should be a draw; I couldn't see anything better. Nevertheless it was clear that I was not in danger, so we moved on to look at more ambitious options for Black.

Next we examined **18...Nd4** 19 Qxf7 Ne6 (threatening to trap the queen with ...Rf8. However, I have . . .) 20 Bg5. (Now Florin Felecan recommended 20...Nxg5, but White is definitely better after 21 Qxg7 Ne6 22 Qh6 Nf4 23 Qg5 Ra5 24 Qg4+ Kd8 25 Rae1 Qxa4 26 Qf3, threatening Qxb7 and Re4. But instead of all this, I think that after . . .) 20...Re8 21 Rfe1 Qf5, Black's pieces are active enough to be able to hold the draw in the endgame.

We also considered 18...Nd4 19 Qxf7 Bf6 as that was an early recommendation of Irina's. But after 20 Ra3, White is better since 20...Ne2+ 21 Kh1 Nxc1 22 Rxc1 Bxb2 does not win material: 23 Re3 gives me the better ending after 23...Qxe3 24 fxe3 Bxc1 25 Qd5.

Then suddenly we saw **18...Bd4**. Wow! 18...Bd4 19 Qxf7 Ne5. Now 20 Qxh7 Ng4 gives Black a huge attack. The main variation we analyzed was: 20 Qb3 Nd3 (this is the point, Black makes a lightning attack on the f2 pawn) 21 Ra3 Nxf2 22 Be3 (instead 22 Rxf2 Qe1 is mate) 22...Ng4 23 Qb5+ Kd8 24 Rf8+ Kc7 (Black's king must tread a delicate path...) 25 Rc3+ Bc5 26 Rxa8 Nxe3 27 Qe2.

This position was also analyzed by the World Team, with the conclusion that White should be better. Incorrect. I suspect they were relying on computers too often in their analysis. A computer would just try to make checks—27...Qb1+ and 28...Qf5+—but they don't work. Instead, Black could play 27...Kd7—with the advantage. White has very little to do, while Black is beautifully coordinated and has a roaring initiative.

There was another possibility for Black after 22 Be3: not ...Ng4 but, 22...Bxe3 23 Qxe3 Qxe3 23 Rxe3 Ng4. I was surprised my opponents considered this to be better for White. I think the ending should be a draw.

I could also vary from the complex line above by playing 26 Bxc5 dxc5 27 Rxc5+ dxc5 28 Qxc5+, forcing a perpetual check—and I would probably have gone for this if 18...Bd4 had been played. We looked for a time at 19 Bd2 to play for a win, but in the end I realized that the consequences would be quite unpredictable. I had already decided that a draw would be a great result for me, and overall a great advertisement for the game of chess itself.

So 18...Bd4 and 18...Nd4 were, in my opinion, very plausible continuations.

We also considered **18...e6**. A solid move. After 19 Qxb6 Nd4, Black certainly has compensation for the slight material disadvantage.

Then Boris called me. "Garry, Khalifman promised a surprise."

"What do you mean, 'a surprise'?"

"I think it is **...f5** because I do not see any other rational move."

"Cmon, ...f5 can't be a good move. I have Bg5. My attack is strong."

"Garry, it's not easy . . ."

So, it seemed that there were four reasonable options for Black, and I don't think any of them were losing. That was an indication of the strength of my opponents' position.

26TH JULY

CROATIA

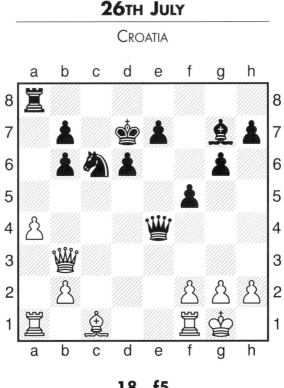

18...f5

> **Analysts' Recommendations:** Krush, 18...f5; Paehtz 18...Nd4;
> Felecan, 18...Nd4; Bacrot, 18...Nd4.
>
> **Voting Results:** 18...f5, 2,639; 18...Nd4, 2,148; 18...e6, 552;
> 18...Ne5, 156; 18...Bd4, 152.

It was the same as before: It seemed my opponents wanted to increase the complexity of the position at every turn. I do not think it is difficult to identify the drawing variations above, but the opposition wanted more.

We realized that 18...f5 was a decision made by an extremely strong player. Alexander Khalifman was behind it. He and his team in St. Petersburg were obviously taking this game very seriously. This aggressive move does not spring easily to mind since you have to be prepared to sacrifice the pawn on b6. Normally, I think it would be difficult to convince the public of the merits of such a move compared to the more straightforward 18...Nd4—as the other analysts recommended—but by this time the Krush bandwagon was rolling. It seemed if she shouted for it, the World Team went for it.

18...f5 is an ambitious continuation: Black safeguards the powerful pawn mass, and even begins to roll it forward a little. What worried me most was that the pawn move added more fuel to the fire: Other moves we considered could lead to a resolution of the position, but this sent a clear message: "The fight goes on!"

We started to look at the position in detail. Boris was trying to get away with **19 Qxb6**, but I didn't even consider it. It was something I just knew would be wrong. It went against my chess principles. After 19...Nd4, White would be put on the defensive immediately: Black threatens ...Ra6 winning the queen, and although it can be extricated, an unpleasant defensive task awaits. In many cases, Black could force the exchange of queens and would still be left with a huge initiative, thanks to the central pawn mass and active pieces. I would have to fight very hard to make a draw.

I felt that the most important rule for me was to keep the queens on the board. If I managed to do that, then I shouldn't lose. It was vital for me to generate some attacking chances against the king on d7 or, at the very least, the potential to create an attack. Without queens, the pawns would be able to roll down the board without endangering the Black king; on the contrary, the king would turn into a mighty supporting player.

27TH JULY

CROATIA

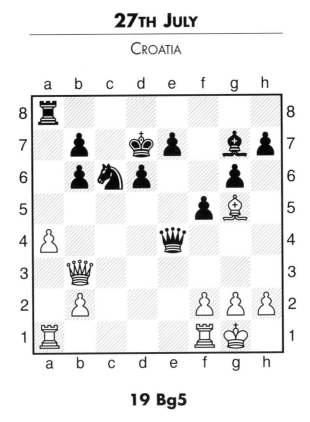

19 Bg5

I did not see all the consequences of Bg5. It was just an intuitive decision: It had to be the right move.

First of all, the bishop moves to the most aggressive square, pressuring the e7 pawn, and at the same time connecting the rooks. That makes Rfe1 possible, attacking Black's queen and increasing the pressure on the e-file. While 18...f5 prevents the pawn from being taken, it does not stop my queen from moving down the diagonal to f7 to hit some tender spots. Nevertheless, the position around Black's king is quite secure as long as the knight stands on c6, so it was not easy to see how I could break through.

Here Black had a choice. One move was 19...Nd4, but I didn't even analyze it; it felt too loose. I mainly considered 19...Qb4 and 19...Qd4.

I was deeply concerned about **19...Qd4**. We spent hours analyzing it. In particular, the line 20 Rfe1 Be5 21 Qf7 Rxa4 22 Rad1 Qxb2 23 Qxh7 Ra2 24 Rf1 Qb3 25 Qxg6 Qe6 troubled us for some time. We were not alone in examining the endgame after 26 Qxe6+ Kxe6 27 Rb1 Bd4 28 Be3 Bc5—"unclear" according to the Krush camp, but White is actually in big trouble. I cannot take on c5: 29 Bxc5 bxc5—it's terrible. Even though white takes on b7, the c and d pawns are just jumping. The h-pawn is not quick enough. Perhaps White could escape, but I would be edging very close to defeat. I was sweating.

Then we found a tremendous resource. Instead of 27 Rb1 I play 27 Rfe1—threatening f4 to win a piece—so Black plays 27...Kf7. And in this position, I play 28 Be3 b5 29 Rd5! b4 30 Rb5!—I stop the pawn and my rook is active. It seemed that White was in no danger of losing. But this endgame is so complicated; and it certainly wasn't the only possibility for Black. For instance, instead of 29...b4, 29...Rb2 is a stronger move, when the position is completely unclear.

In fact, it seems that I underestimated my chances again. After 19...Qd4 20 Rae1, White can develop tangible attacking chances. Black must prevent the queen check on e6: 20...Be5, and now 21 Kh1! threatens to use the f-pawn to batter open the e-file again. The power of White's attack is shown in the line 21...h6? 22 Bxe7! Nxe7 23 f4 Qxb2 (23...Bf6 24 Qe6+ Kc7 25 Rd1 wins) 24 Qf7 Rxa4 25 fxe5 dxe5 26 Rb1 (26 Rg1!? is also good) 26...Rf4 27 Rg1 Qf2 28 Qf6. With the cover around Black's king disappearing, it will be very difficult to quell White's initiative.

After 19...Qd4 20 Rae1 Be5 21 Kh1, it is better to play 21...Qxb2, though White still has the better chances after 22 Qf7 Bf6 (22...Rxa4 23 Qxh7 Qc2 24 Qxg6 is a little better for White) 23 Rb1 Qd4 24 Rfd1 Ne5 (if 24...Qc3 25 Bf4! Be5 26 Be3 Ra4 27 Qh7, all White's pieces are involved in the attack—compare with the game) 25 Rxd4 Nxf7 26 Bxf6 exf6 27 Rxb6 Kc7. White has managed to inflict some damage on Black's wonderful pawn structure.

At the time I looked at many other variations besides this to find an answer to 19...Qd4, without coming up with anything that was completely satisfactory. However, when the analysts' recommendations appeared, it turned out that Bacrot was the only one who was advocating it, so the chances of the World Team going for it was slim. Krush was recommending 19...Qb4, while Paehtz and Felecan went for 19...Nd4. I was convinced the knight move was a mistake. I immediately called Tel Aviv.

"Boris, I smell something here. I don't see how exactly, but I feel they should lose. Put a computer onto it."

Why did I have my suspicions about this knight move? Very simply, because minor pieces need solid protection, usually by a pawn. In the main variation below, it is not just the knight which loses its anchor, but the bishop too, and that has to be dubious. In 1977, when I was fourteen years old, I remember adjourning a game an exchange down—I had rook and bishop against my opponent's two rooks—but the situation was still rather unclear.

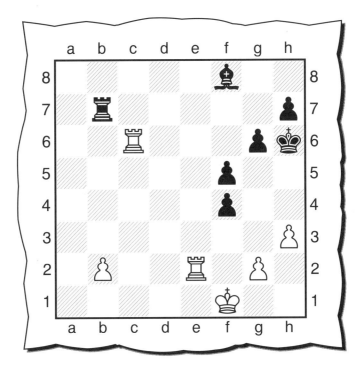

Zaid–Kasparov, USSR, 1977

I telephoned my mentor, the former world champion Mikhail Botvinnik, for some advice. "Garry, just tell me one thing, is your bishop protected by a pawn?" The answer was no. "Then you are lost." He didn't even need to look at the exact position, he just knew from that that I was in trouble. And he was right; I did indeed lose the adjournment. It was a painful, but invaluable, lesson to learn.

Just over an hour later, Boris called me back. "Garry Kimovich, a forced eleven move line. They are lost."

The main line runs: 20 Qf7 Ne2+ 21 Kh1 Bxb2 (Black escapes temporarily, but neither Elisabeth or Florin found the next move) 22 Ra2! (Black's problem is that there are too many points and pieces that need defending: the bishop, the knight and the pawn on e7) 22...Bd4 (22...Bc3 23 f3 Qe5 24 Qc4! traps the knight on e2) 23 f3 Qe5 24 Bh4 (threatening Re1—the bishop protects the rook, so preventing ...Ng3+) 24...Bc3 25 Qc4 Nf4 26 Bg5 Ne6 27 Re2 Rc8 28 Qa2! Nxg5 (Black must give up the queen and hope to build a fortress, however...) 29 Rxe5 Bxe5 30 a5! (30 f4 Bxf4—back-rank—wouldn't be too clever) 30...bxa5 31 f4 Bxf4 32 Qa4+ (that's the difference!) and Qxf4.

A long line, and there are alternative defenses, but after the crucial move 22 Ra2! Black is only hanging on by a byte—and in the end that isn't sufficient.

A computer is an enormous help in positions like this where there are forcing variations. But this was not simply the work of a computer. A machine can't see anything through to the finish itself—you have to guide it, and at this, Boris is expert.

We checked the line thoroughly. Then we waited.

28TH JULY

CROATIA

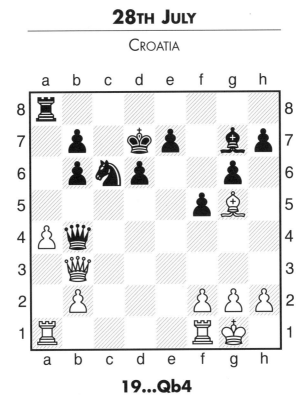

19...Qb4

> **Analysts' Recommendations:** Krush, 19...Qb4; Paehtz, 19...Nd4;
> Felecan, 19...Nd4; Bacrot, 19...Qd4.
>
> **Voting Results:** 19...Qb4, 2,347; 19...Nd4, 2,264; 19...Qd4, 875;
> 19...h6, 216; 19...Bd4, 133.

At around 3:30 PM—6:30 AM on the U.S. west coast—when all the votes had been collated in Seattle and were available for my inspection, everyone who was in the house gathered in our work room in the basement to watch as I went online. The game could be decided in a moment.

I was sure it was going to be a close vote—and I was right. There was just over 1 percent in it, 83 votes, to be precise, but unfortunately not in my favor. 19...Qb4 just scraped through. It was a letdown for everyone.

As I said before, 19...Qb4 wasn't the move I feared the most, but it was still good. As usual, I could not contemplate exchanging queens, so I had to move away from my queenside pawns; but on a positive note I could attack

Black's kingside pawns and the pawn on e7 by sliding down to f7.

It was quite clear to me now what a well-managed team I was facing. When Irina made her recommendation, she did not include a proper analysis of 19...Nd4; instead she concentrated on her own move, 19...Qb4, and the major alternative, 19...Qd4. Then when the Smart Chess team saw two of the other experts recommending 19...Nd4, they sensed there could be trouble.

They understood that a move that grabbed a pawn and had no obvious refutation would be enormously tempting for voters. So they bent the rules again. They found a mistake with 19...Nd4 and published it on the Smart Chess website while the vote was in progress. And there was a link to their site from the Microsoft Gaming Zone.

Again, it was not 100 percent correct or ethical, but there was no direct violation of the rules: I repeat, this analysis was on their own site, not Microsoft's. However, it might have been enough to change the tide of opinion by just 1 percent.

It seemed odd to me that there was a direct link from the Microsoft game site to Smart Chess. I suppose Microsoft agreed to this out of a sense of obligation as the analysts were not being paid for their work; they were just doing it for the publicity. It could hardly have been foreseen that this link would be used to influence the course of the game. This episode felt like a serious breach of etiquette, and I took it badly.

All this time I was in Croatia I should have been preparing for my match against Anand. We did manage to do some analysis for that match. I didn't leave Croatia empty-handed, but I have to say that the Microsoft game was a huge handicap. To create good ideas you need the right state of mind, and the situation I was in was not ideal.

The game was consuming too much of my mental energy. I was becoming anxious. I realized that my goal of finishing the game, or at least of having a position where the moves came automatically by the time I left Croatia on August 22nd, was just a dream. Should I have offered a draw to cut the game short? No. I never considered offering a draw. For me it was a real game and I wanted to play it out to its natural conclusion. If it finally ended in a draw, then I would have to accept it, but until then I would fight. Besides, what if my draw offer had been turned down? It would have been just too embarrassing to contemplate.

29TH JULY

CROATIA

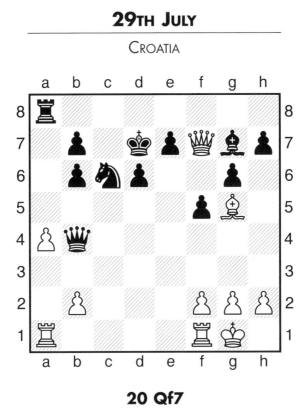

20 Qf7

I avoid the exchange of queens, attack the bishop, and line up pressure on Black's e7 pawn—though for now it is guarded by the knight on c6.

I had to play 20 Qf7, but anyway, I was glad to threaten something, to create a little confusion in the enemy ranks. Black has to decide what to do about the bishop. Capturing the pawn on b2 with either queen or bishop must have tempted some players, but neither is terribly good. **20...Bxb2** would allow a nasty pin: 21 Rab1. Black could escape from it, but it would be time consuming. And **20...Qxb2** also allows me to gain time with 21 Rab1 and then I can build up pressure against the e-pawn with Rfe1. To be honest, I didn't even consider these captures. They were obviously not the strongest moves, so I didn't waste my time on them.

On July 30, the FIDE knockout tournament was due to start in Las Vegas, which meant that from this day, Alexander Khalifman had more pressing matters to attend to than analyzing the game. I doubt if he realized that his most loyal supporters in the tournament were in our house in Croatia. Every morning we would check the results from Las Vegas to see if he had made it through another round, and on each of those mornings I would arrive back upstairs for breakfast and salute his victory, "Khalif is genius!"

Each match Khalifman won in Las Vegas prolonged his absence from the Microsoft game by another day, depriving the World Team of one of its shrewdest advisers.

"I would love to be able to say that because I am the number one chess player in the world, it means that I have all the answers. It does not. It only means that, most of the time, I can steer my way through the complexities of this baffling game better than anyone else. Chess has not yet revealed all its secrets, and perhaps never will."

—Garry Kasparov

30TH JULY

CROATIA

20...Be5

> **Analysts' Recommendations:** Krush, 20...Be5; Paehtz, 20...Be5; Felecan, 20...Be5; Bacrot, 20...Be5.
>
> **Voting Results:** 20...Be5, 5,334; 20...Qxb2, 615; 20...Bxb2, 494; 20...Qd4, 144; 20...Bd4, 90.

This is the best way of dealing with the threat to the bishop: It moves away from the queen and blocks the e-file. I cannot capture the pawn with **21 Qxh7** as 21...Rh8 wins: the queen moves and the bishop crashes in on h2. However, I could threaten to take on h7 by playing **21 h3**, solving the problem on the h-file.

There were other tempting possibilities. I could try to pursue my attack by playing 21 f4 to open the e-file; or 21 Rac1 to sacrifice on c6 so as to break through on e7.

Let's deal with **21 f4** first. There is no need for Black to give a check on d4—that can be saved for a really important moment—so 21...Bxb2 is now correct. 22 Rae1 Qxa4! 23 Qe6+ Kc7 24 Bxe7 Bd4+ 25 Kh1 Nxe7 26 Qxe7+ Qd7 27 Qh4 Re8 28 Rxe8 Qxe8 29 Qxh7+ Kc6. In my opinion Black has the upper hand: The king's exposure is just an illusion. His majesty will be covered by the advancing queenside pawns.

The move 21 f4 has certain positional shortcomings: it cuts off the bishop on g5 from the other side of the board; it weakens all the squares in the middle of the board; and White's attacking chances are immediately reduced to just one option—destroying the pawn on e7. A move like that must win instantly. If it doesn't, then you are out of business. From the beginning I had my doubts about f4, so after an initial investigation proved inconclusive, I spent no more time on it.

21 Rac1 was worth a more thorough look. The main line I considered runs: 21...Rxa4 22 Qxh7 (22 Rxc6 bxc6 23 Qxe7+ Kc8 24 Qe8+ Ke7 25 Qd7+ Ka6 26 Qxc6 Qe4 27 Qd7 should not be worse for Black with such well-centralized pieces) 22...Qg4 23 b3! (that stops Black from blocking with the rook on the c-file in a couple of moves) 23...Rb4 24 Rxc6 Kxc6 25 Rc1+ Kb5 26 Qxg6 Rxb3 27 Qe8+ Kb4. In spite of the Black king's enforced tour of the board, the situation remains anything but clear.

Of course, if this wasn't quite to Black's taste, there were alternatives en route: 21...Qxa4, for instance. I couldn't actually see my way through all the complications, and I was concerned that I could suddenly find myself in a situation where there was no way out for me.

The game continued to create a tense atmosphere in the house. July 30th was Yulia's birthday, and she wanted me to cut my study time. I did my best, but I was late for my rendezvous with her and Vadim at the local funfair, with predictable consequences.

Family life creates additional pressures for everyone, but especially for a chess player who does not work set hours in the day. When one marries, it takes time and energy to adjust one's lifestyle, and that often affects a chess player's results. And of course children add to the confusion, too. I have been lucky to cope with these changes well. My wife and I have a good understanding, but it can be difficult nonetheless if I have to travel to a tournament, or, in this case, if I have to spend an extra hour analyzing. It is a constant fight for balance.

The reason I was late for the rendezvous was because we were having one last look at 21 h3. I wasn't completely happy with it, but in the end I couldn't see anything better.

31ST JULY

CROATIA

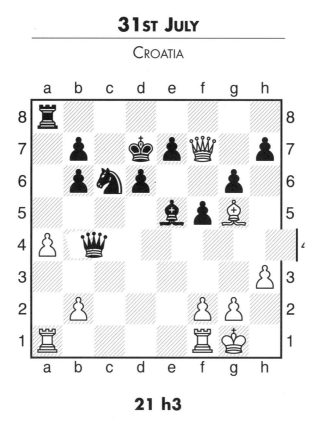

21 h3

As my attacking attempts didn't convince me, I fell back on the idea of safeguarding my king position, with the aim of taking Black's kingside pawns. Now Black had some choice.

On the bulletin boards **21...Rh8** was discussed in great detail, though I am not sure why. It simply looks too passive. After 22 Rad1 Qxb2 23 Rfe1, Black is on the verge of losing.

The move that had concerned me the day before was **21...f4**, cutting off my bishop from the other side of the board. Then 22 Qxh7 Qe4 23 Qf7 Qf5 forces an endgame that is finely balanced, but easier for Black to play than White. My bishop is cut off, Black controls the center, Black's minor pieces are well placed, my queenside pawns are weak. . . In other words, the same old story.

In fact, after 21...f4 I would probably have played 22 Rac1, which leads to fresh complications. For example: 22...Qxa4, and now White could sacrifice immediately: 23 Rxc6 Kxc6 24 Rc1+ Kb5 25 Qd5+ Ka6 26 Bxe7, with a great initiative, though Black has two extra pawns. Verdict: unclear.

Instead of sacrificing, White could play a very tricky move: 23 Rc4. If 23...Qb5, then 24 Rxc6 really is powerful: 24...bxc6 25 Qxe7+ Kc8 26 Qe8+ Kb7 27 Qf7+ Kb8 28 Qg8+ Kb7 (the king cannot move to the a-file as Ra1+ would win, so is caught while White picks up as many pawns as possible) 29 Qxh7+ Kb8 30 Qg8+ Kb7 31 Qf7 + Kb8 32 Bxf4. White has a clear advantage due to the poor position of Black's king.

After 21...f4 22 Rac1 Qxa4 23 Rc4, it is better to play 23...Rf8. Exchanging rooks wouldn't help White, but the ending is an improvement on many of the others we have looked at so far in this game: 24 Qxe7+ Nxe7 25 Rxa4. At least one of Black's dangerous center pawns has gone. Chances are balanced.

1ST AUGUST

CROATIA

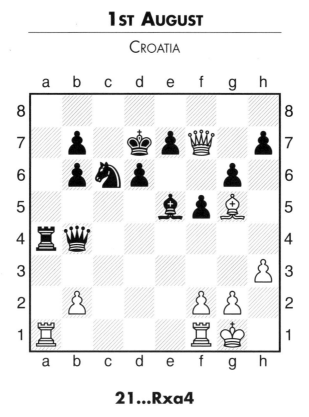

21...Rxa4

> **Analysts' Recommendations:** Krush, 21...Rxa4; Paehtz, 21...Rxa4; Felecan, 21...Rh8; Bacrot, 21...Rxa4.
>
> **Voting Results:** 21...Ra4, 3,422; 21...Rh8, 746; 21...Qxb2, 150; 21...Bxb2, 130; 21...f4, 90.

Now I had to decide whether to go in for an exchange of pieces, or attempt to rekindle my attack with **22 Rac1**. Once again, the idea is to capture the knight on c6, which protects the pawn on e7. However, here, this would really only be a drawing attempt.

The move could have its merits in practical chess, but it is out of place in this kind of game. On the last turn I had already rejected the murky idea of moving the rook to c1, so I did so again: I could not afford to make a decision without being able to foresee all the consequences. My fear was that I could quite easily lose control of the position, and then suddenly it might be too late to hold the game. My instincts told me that I was not out of danger, so I had to play as correctly as possible. It was still my goal to limit the damage so that I wouldn't lose. I didn't mind drawing. I felt I was up against a worthy team.

I could now foresee that this game was going to last for a very long time. Not only had it eaten into my preparation time for the match against Anand, but the way events on the board were unfolding, it was going to run into the very match itself. I was concerned, so I asked Microsoft to introduce multiple move options so as to speed up the game.

So-called "conditional continuations" are well known in correspondence chess. If there is a sequence of forced moves, usually captures, then one side or the other can offer that string of moves to be played out at one go to save time. In this game, for example, after 21...Rxa4, both sides knew well in advance that the position after 24 Qxg6 was going to be reached. We could have played the moves out at one go and so saved ourselves about a week in the process.

In the end Microsoft decided against it. For them, the primary purpose of this game was to entertain, and speeding up the procedure would confuse the less serious players for whom a move a day was the perfect pace for understanding the subtleties of the game. A rhythm had already been established, and they were reluctant to change it for fear of a negative reaction. No matter how automatic a move seemed, some players might feel they were being "hustled."

My point was that this game had long ceased to be an event where ordinary players could have their say. Everyone was following the suggestions from Irina and her group. It had turned into a tough professional game, and I did not like the pretense that it was otherwise.

2ND AUGUST

CROATIA

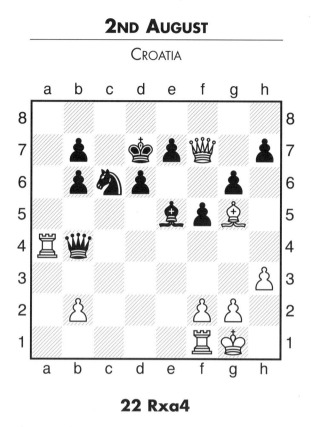

22 Rxa4

After this, the next few moves are forced. I exchange rooks, and take two pawns on Black's kingside, matching the two pawns I am losing on the queenside.

3RD AUGUST

CROATIA

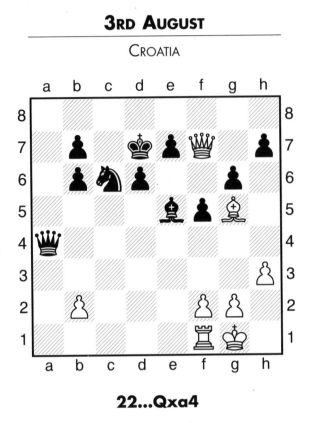

22...Qxa4

Analysts' Recommendations: Krush, 22...Qxa4; Paehtz, 22...Qxa4; Felecan, 22...Qxa4; Bacrot, 22...Qxa4.

Voting Results: 22...Qxa4, 7,031; 22...Qxb2, 27; 22...Nd8, 21; 22...Qb5, 9; 22...d5, 8.

Black recaptures the rook: absolutely forced.

4TH AUGUST

CROATIA

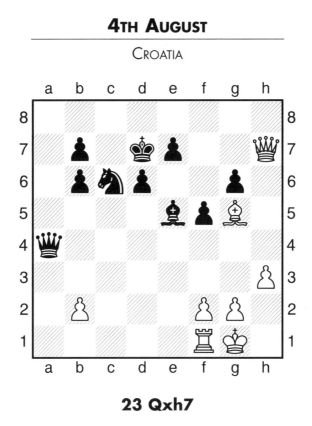

23 Qxh7

I begin my harvest of Black's pawns.

5TH AUGUST

CROATIA

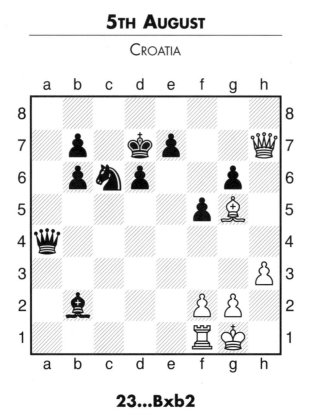

23...Bxb2

Analysts' Recommendations: Krush, 23...Bxb2; Paehtz, 23...Bxb2; Felecan, 23...Bxb2; Bacrot, 23...Bxb2.

Voting Results: 23...Bxb2, 6,025; 23...Qe4, 112; 23...Qc4, 78; 23...f4, 63; 23...Qb5, 61.

My last pawn on the queenside disappears. It doesn't pose an immediate danger for me, but it is funny to think that in the end, both the b- and the d-pawn made the long journey down the board to transform into queens. Luckily for me, my h-pawn succeeded, too.

6TH AUGUST

CROATIA

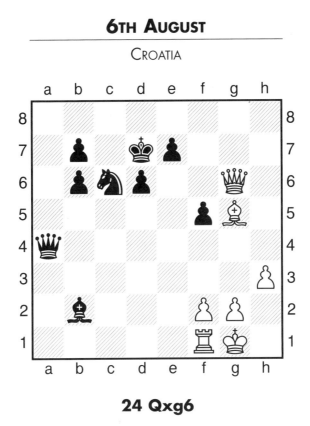

24 Qxg6

I reply in kind by capturing the g-pawn, and at the same time threaten the f-pawn, which Black must defend.

7TH AUGUST

CROATIA

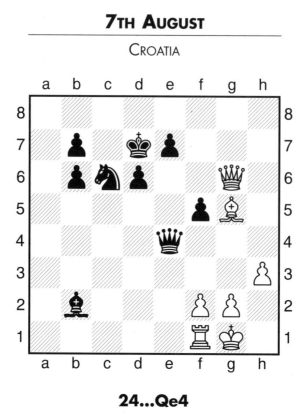

24...Qe4

> **Analysts' Recommendations:** Krush, 24...Qe4; Paehtz, 24...Qe4; Felecan, 24...Qe4; Bacrot, 24...Qe4.
>
> **Voting Results:** 24...Qe4, 5,076; 24...Nd4, 138; 24...Qc2, 93; 24...Ne5, 89; 24...f4, 55.

This was undoubtedly the best move. The pawn on f5 was threatened, so the queen moved over to protect it; and at the same time it returned to the center of the board, preventing White's rook from occupying the e1 square. A classic case of centralization.

The position has stabilized again after the turbulence of the last few moves. Taking a straight piece count, there is still a dynamic balance between the two armies: Black has a knight and two pawns against White's rook, so in that respect there is a rough equality. Therefore, it is necessary to look at other factors to understand what is going on.

Both sides have passed pawns. (A passed pawn is one whose path to the other side of the board is not obstructed by opposing pawns.) I have a passed h-pawn; and the World has passed b-pawns and a passed d-pawn. As more pieces are exchanged, the power and influence of these passed pawns increases, as it becomes easier for them to move down the board.

On paper, White's queen, rook and bishop should be worth more than the queen, knight and bishop, but at the moment Black's pieces are far more actively placed: the queen on e4 and the bishop on the long diagonal dominate.

A few moves back I thought this position was much better for White, but Boris, as usual, did a very good job of curbing my optimism. Lines such as **25 h4** b5 26 h5 Bd4 27 h6 b4 28 Qf7 d5 29 h7 b3 convinced me that I could actually be in serious trouble if I didn't take care: The b-pawn has no obstacles. This final position demonstrates all the strengths of Black's position, chiefly, the centralized queen, and the centralized bishop controlling h8 and b2. And all the while White's rook is stuck on f1 like a spectator watching the racing pawns.

Pushing the h-pawn was the most straightforward idea, but the consequences were at best unclear, and at worst downright bad. I had been in a similar situation a few moves earlier. It was vital that I kept control of the position so that I could see what was coming over the horizon. If I didn't, the consequences could be fatal.

In light of the variation above, I decided the b-pawn had to be stopped.

8TH AUGUST

CROATIA

25 Qf7

The queen maintains the pressure on the e7 pawn, preventing Black's queen and knight from straying too far, and if necessary it can retreat to b3, preventing the b-pawn from advancing. This was another tense moment in the game.

At first, Krush and her followers indicated on the bulletin boards that they wanted to play **25...d5** here, to cut off my queen's retreat. It took them a long time to find the reply 26 Rd1. After 26...Bd4 27 Kf1! White threatens Re1, guaranteeing that the rook comes into play on the e-file. Nevertheless, Black can still hold the balance in this position. The main line runs:

27...b5 28 Re1 Qd3+ 29 Kg1 Bc5 30 Qe6+ Kc7 31 Bf4+ Kb6 32 Qd7. And now, when it looks as though White is closing in for the kill, Black has 32...e5! 33 Bxe5 Nxe5 34 Rxe5 Bxf2+! 35 Kxf2 Qd4+ 36 Re3 f4 37 Qd6+, and the game ends in perpetual check.

Then we found another draw for Black, but this time much clearer, beginning with the powerful move **25...Nd4**. The principal idea is contained in the following variation:

26 h4 Ne2+ 27 Kh1 Bc3! 28 h5 Bd2! (the bishop cannot be captured because of Qh4 mate) 29 Qg7 (protecting the bishop) 29...Bc3 30 Qf7 (if 30 Qg6 Qd3! threatening ...Ng3+, and the rook does not have a safe square to move to along the first rank) 30...Bd2 with a draw by repetition.

In this line, Irina and Co. were concerned about the ending after 29 Bxe7 Qxe7 30 Qxf5+ Qe6 31 Qxe6+ Kxe6 32 Rb1. However, this is a dead draw: 32...Nc3! 33 Rxb6 Ne4 34 Kg1 Nf6 rounds up the h-pawn.

Unfortunately, poor Florin Felecan missed his big day. Earlier, it seemed as though he had wanted to play the knight to d4 at every opportunity; but here, when it would have really counted, he recommended putting the bishop there instead.

9TH AUGUST

CROATIA

25...Bd4

Analysts' Recommendations: Krush, 25...Bd4; Paehtz, 25...d5; Felecan, 25...Bd4; Bacrot, 25...Bd4.

Voting Results: 25...Bd4, 3758; 25...d5, 486; 25...Nd4, 213; 25...b5, 209; 25...Be5, 181.

When Irina and her team recommended 25...Bd4 instead of 25...Nd4, I realized they wanted to increase the pressure rather than make a draw. In their analysis of 25...Nd4, they gave some lines trying to prove that White was better, but their reasoning simply did not hang together. I would have had no choice but to go for a draw.

That is not to say that 25...Bd4 is a poor move. Black pre-empts the queen's retreat and places the bishop on a safe central square, protecting the b6 pawn and pressurizing the f2 square.

By now, I was finding the position so complex that, even with the help of a computer, it was impossible to figure out all the variations. Therefore, to help to illuminate a path through this forest, I attempted to formulate some general principles for the position.

I had already achieved one small victory in my fight back: exchanging a pair of rooks. In general, when playing the exchange down, minor pieces do not operate as well without the support of a rook.

Yet I still had the problem that my rook was not participating in the struggle. I also wanted to advance my h-pawn, but it was too far away from the queening square, and, as we saw in an earlier variation, it is difficult to get it past the Black bishop, dominant on the long diagonal.

It was clear that I had two main aims: to exchange the bishops, and to activate the rook. To free my rook so that it could better participate in the action, I realized that it might be helpful to exchange queens, so that became a secondary target.

Any change in the position affects your aims. Whereas earlier I was not interested in a queen exchange, now it became more attractive to me. Why? Because Black's minor pieces work best with the support of a rook—and that rook had just been exchanged from the board.

Having understood these principles, my next move became much clearer.

Around this time news came of my forthcoming world championship match against Anand. Bad news. It would either be postponed or perhaps even cancelled altogether. It was a heavy blow as only the year before my match with Shirov had also fallen through. I had great faith in Bessel Kok, but it seemed that even he could not secure the deal we were looking for.

A combination of factors had discouraged the sponsor. First, we were simply too late with our bid. Second, the package we put forward, which included the establishment of a permanent qualification cycle for future matches, was just too ambitious. And third, there was an imbalance in the strength of the players. It might have been a match between the world's number 1 and 2, but the sponsor kept asking, "Why should we put up $3 million when everyone knows who will win?" Apart from draws, my career record against Anand was thirteen wins and only three losses; and in our world championship match in New York in 1995, I beat him quite convincingly.

(A few months later my agent, Owen Williams, made a grim joke before I began Wijk-aan-Zee 2000—"Garry, perhaps it would be for the best if you had a bad tournament." There was a grain of truth in what he said. In spite of his advice, I won the event. Nevertheless, it is looking likely that I will defend my title against Vladimir Kramnik in October 2000, and in classical chess we have a level record: forgetting the draws, we have had three wins and three losses apiece.)

The news affected my preparation badly. When there is a goal ahead of you, apart from the actual study on the board, one's mind is working the whole time on sharp variations, even subconsciously. When the goal disappears, the mental urgency goes, too.

A reappraisal of my situation was necessary. I reasoned that I might not be playing a world championship match, but I was playing the most amazing game against the World, a game that would probably be remembered long after many others I would play. It was compensation for not having the match. So I resolved to take the game seriously, and to do my very best to win.

10TH AUGUST

CROATIA

26 Qb3

The queen prevents the dangerous b-pawn from advancing, and at the same time rejoins her comrades. With her help it would be easier to achieve my objectives of activating the rook and exchanging bishops.

Most of the analysis on the bulletin boards and from Smart Chess was centered on **26...Bc5**. This was in fact Irina's original suggestion. For instance, 27 Qb1 was suggested, but after 27...d5! 28 Qxe4 fxe4, the position is very unclear. It is not easy for White's pawns to advance, but Black's, on the other hand, can march through the center. If necessary the king goes to e6 and f5 to support the pawns and stop the h-pawn. I did not think Black had the worse position.

However, after 26...Bc5 I was amazed that no one considered 27 Qd1! with the idea Re1, pushing the queen from the powerful square on e4. For instance:

27 ..b5 28 Re1 Qc4 29 Qf3 e6 30 Bf6! Qc2 (30...b4 31 Qh5 is good for White) 31 h4! b4 32 h5 b3 33 h6 b2 34 h7 and wins. This is a nice mirror of the variation at move 24 where it was Black who controlled the

long diagonal and was able to force a pawn home. This time White's bishop occupies the diagonal, and the result flips to fit.

Not that that was Black's best defense. 27...e5 is a better try, so that White's bishop cannot claim the long diagonal, as above. Nevertheless, it does expose Black's king a little: 28 Qh5 Nd4 29 Qf7+ Kc6 30 Qe8+ Kd5. Mad. Though how I exploit the king's strange position is another matter. It is too well protected. Nevertheless, I would have the comfortable choice between making a draw or staying in the fight. In other words, the tide of the game would have turned.

After 26...Bc5 I would not be winning; Objectively, I wouldn't even have the advantage, but I would certainly have been out of risk, and I could even think about taking over the initiative. Since move 10 it felt as though I had been on the defensive, and here was my chance. I considered that 26...Bc5 was fundamentally wrong: In a position where I have a passed h-pawn, the bishop has to remain on the long diagonal.

But then at the last moment I found **26...f4**—an excellent move—and unfortunately, the opposition did, too.

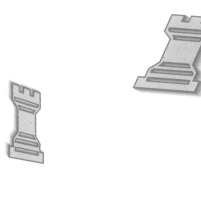

11TH AUGUST

CROATIA

26...f4

> **Analysts' Recommendations:** Krush, 26...f4; Paehtz, 26...Bc5; Felecan, 26...Bc5; Bacrot, 26...Bc5.
>
> **Voting Results:** 26...f4, 2,631; 26...Bc5, 2,602; 26...Na5, 206; 26...e6, 127; 26...Ne5, 118.

Amazing. It felt like the World Team was ahead of us in their analysis again.

The vote was incredibly close, hardly surprising, since for several days 26...Bc5 had been analyzed on the bulletin boards, and the three analysts, apart from Irina, all recommended the bishop move.

Nevertheless, the World chose to go with Irina's ambitious recommendation 26...f4. The principal aim of nudging the pawn forward is to lock the bishop on g5 out of the game. This prevents me from returning the bishop to e3, for instance, initiating an exchange—one of my aims.

Just compare the bishops: Black's, on d4, controls many more squares than its counterpart on g5. My bishop, stuck out on g5, attacks the pawns on f4 and e7, but they can both be taken care of. Apart from that, its scope is limited: With the pawn on f4, my bishop can only operate on one side of the board.

Smart Chess's decision to play 26...f4 was highly professional, and I have to praise them for that. They knew that I could now force a draw with 27 Qf7 Be5 28 Qb3, etc., but they appreciated that trying to avoid this continuation could lead them into trouble.

I do not know who was originally behind the move 26...f4, and who conducted the analysis of it. Perhaps it was Irina, but I have my doubts; there are no miracles in the world of chess. I even saw some people saying on the bulletin boards that Bobby Fischer was involved! That stretches belief, but there was obviously someone recommending these moves and orchestrating the program of analysis who had a great knowledge of the game of chess. I could see by the depth, but also difference in style of the Smart Chess analysis, that many people were involved in the work. I suppose they had so many supporters that variations could be checked very easily, then analysis sent back to HQ.

All the same, there was no doubt that our analysis was of a better quality—much of theirs relied too heavily on computers—but they had greater quantity; and with the help of skillful management, they succeeded in converting this quantity into quality.

After 26...f4 the game started again.

Kasparov Against the World

12TH AUGUST

CROATIA

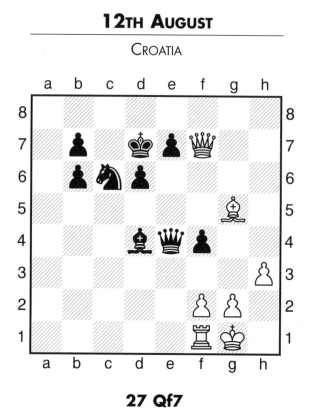

27 Qf7

Attacking the f-pawn. There is no alternative here. I had to give my bishop a role again, and besides that, 26...f4 slightly weakened the light-squares, exposing the king. It is natural for my queen to return to f7.

13TH AUGUST

CROATIA

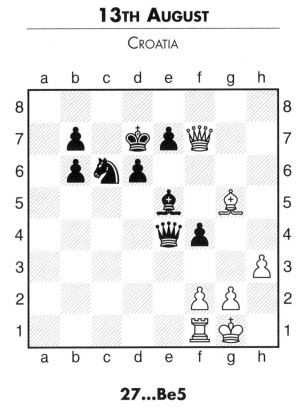

27...Be5

The only sensible way of meeting the threat to the f-pawn. 27...f3 was considered on the bulletin boards, but I don't see the point: 28 gxf3 wins a pawn and my king is still quite safe.

After 27...Be5, I was seriously tempted to force a draw by returning with my queen to b3, attacking the pawn on b6. After **28 Qb3**, even if Black wants to play 28...Kc7, then I could still play 29 Qf7 to get a draw, or, more ambitiously, 29 Qe6. In all likelihood, the point would be split after 28...Bd4 29 Qf7, etc.

I had a dilemma. After all, a few moves ago, I felt I was in such trouble that it had merely been my aim to survive, and now if I wanted to I could actually force a draw! Owen Williams spoke to Eddie Ranchigoda, the manager at Microsoft responsible for running the game, to see if he had a preference. Eddie's attitude was neutral. It was completely up to me.

I discussed the situation with Yuri and Boris. True to form, Yuri wanted to go for the kill, whereas Boris was more cautious. He couldn't make up his mind.

In the end I thought that playing 28 Qb3 would be cowardly. It was time to show character. If the game finally ended in a draw, then so be it, but I wanted to see what would happen first. I had escaped from my earlier difficulties, and although I didn't believe I was winning (in fact, I didn't even see that I had any advantage), I thought it was safe enough to play on.

14TH AUGUST

CROATIA

28 h4

It had taken a long time to arrange this pawn's advance, and it wasn't clear how much further it was going to go. Forcing it through to the eighth rank was not going to be at all easy, particularly while that bishop was sitting on the e5 square, dominating the long diagonal. For the time being I had to postpone my plan of activating the rook on f1—there was no safe square for it to land on.

15TH AUGUST

CROATIA

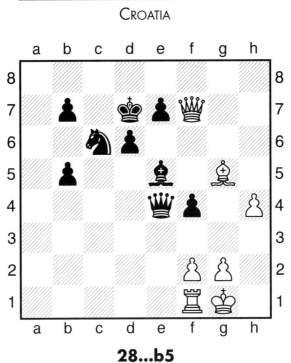

28...b5

> **Analysts' Recommendations:** Krush, 28...b5; Paehtz, 28...b5; Felecan, 28...b5; Bacrot, 28...b5.
>
> **Voting Results:** 28...b5, 3891; 28...f3, 183; 28...d5, 89; 28...Nd8, 88; 28...Kc8, 57.

I realized that my opponents were intending to play ...Qc4 to help advance the b-pawn, so I briefly considered the preventative **29 Rc1**, but Black has a very simple solution. The rook suddenly feels exposed away from the protection of the king, so why not attack it? 29...Bb2. White's best response is probably just to go back to f1 and repeat the position, for if 30 Rd1 Nd4 31 h5 f3 32 g3 b4, to add to the usual problems, White's king is poorly placed.

16TH AUGUST

CROATIA

29 h5

In this position there were three main moves that had to be considered: 29...Qc4 (played in the game); 29...Qe2; and 29...b4.

29...Qe2 was a strong move. After 30 Bxf4 Bxf4 31 Qxf4 Qxh5, an unbalanced ending arises, which the Smart Chess team thought would give White the better chances. I disagree. Black's king is securely protected by the knight and pawns; the b-pawn provides counter play; and from my point of view, it is extremely difficult to advance the pawns on the kingside without exposing my king.

For example:

32 Qe3! White's best chance is to try to break into Black's fortress, but Black covers the entry square on b6 with 32 ..Kc7. White can attempt to break through by maneuvering, or by advancing pawns on the kingside. First, a pawn move:

33 f4 (threat: f4-f5-f6, exchanging pawns and so creating a weakness on d6. But the queen blocks firmly) 33...Qf5 34 Rc1 (threat: Qxe7+) 34...Kb8 35 Qb6 (threat: Rxc6) 35...Qd5 (Black remains rock solid, so White tries a

distraction) 36 f5 Qxf5 37 Rxc6 Qb1+ 38 Kh2 Qh7+. Black didn't need to capture the f-pawn, but why not? It's a draw by perpetual check. Advancing the f-pawn inflicts more weaknesses on White's position than Black's.

Alternatively, White could hope to get in just by using the queen and rook: 33 Rc1 (threat: Qxe7+) 33...Qh4 34 g3 Qf6 35 Rd1 b4 36 Rd5 (a crafty maneuver to get the rook to b5—an idea we have already come across in a variation to White's nineteenth move—but Black is able to defend) 36...Qa1+ 37 Kg2 Qa4 38 Qd3 Kb6, once again preventing the rook from landing on b5 and threatening to advance the b-pawn.

Both sides have so many plausible moves that the only possible verdict on the ending is unclear. With best play I imagine a draw should be the correct result.

Bacrot actually recommended going for this ending via the move order 29...Qc4 30 Qf8 (in the game I played 30 Qf5+) 30...Qe2 31 Qf5+ Kc7 32 Bxf4 Bxf4 33 Qxf4 Qxh5, even though he too considered that White would have the better chances.

Etienne Bacrot was by far the strongest player among the analysts, and sometimes his recommendations were excellent. However, he was obviously not spending very long over the game, so in positions that required concentration and calculation, he often did badly. At other moments, when he could use his fine positional judgement, he did much better. It was a pity for the World Team that no one knew when to listen to him.

After 29...Qe2, instead of heading for the ending, I could try 30 Qf5+, which tests Black, though in the end I found a clear way to draw. Here is just the main line; the conclusion is rather pretty:

30...Kc7 31 Qh3 (this is the idea, to put the queen behind the h-pawn, giving its advance more force) 31...Qc2 32 Qg4! (32 h6 Qg6! is still very complicated, but satisfactory for Black) 32...b4! 33 Bxf4 Qe4 34 g3 b3 (it's the old story—Black's queen and bishop control the central diagonals, so the b-pawn is more dangerous than the h; White must challenge Black's dominance) 35 Qg6! Qxg6 36 hxg6 Bg7 37 Rb1 b2 38 Kf1 Na5 39 Ke2 Nc4 40 Kd3 Na3 (Black gets there first, but...) 41 Rxb2! Bxb2 42 Bc1! and the bishop ending after 42...Bg7 43 Bxa3 will end in a draw.

The most straightforward move, **29...b4**, had to be considered carefully, though with best play it leads Black to an inferior version of the queen and knight versus queen and rook ending considered above. For instance: 30 h6

Qc2 31 Bxf4 Nd8 32 Qh5 Bxf4 33 h7 Be5 34 Qxe5 dxe5 35 h8Q Nc6 (35...b3 36 Qxe5 Nc6 37 Qd5+ Kc7 38 Qd1 Qc3 39 Qc1 is clearly better for White) 36 Qh3+ Kc7 37 Qe3. Having recentralized the queen, the b-pawn has been prevented from advancing, and White is ready to activate the rook on c1. The doubled e-pawn makes a huge difference to the position: Black's king is less secure, and the knight is less likely to move from its spot as the pawn on e5 needs protection. It isn't easy to win, but there is no doubting who has the better chances: White.

Anyway, all this was suggested. Instead of 29...Qe2 or 29...b4, the World voted resoundingly for 29...Qc4.

17TH AUGUST

CROATIA

29...Qc4

Analysts' Recommendations: Krush, 29...Qc4; Paehtz, 29...Qc4; Felecan, 29...Qc4; Bacrot, 29...Qc4.

Voting Results: 29...Qc4, 4,796; 29...b4, 353; 29...f3, 218; 29...Qe2, 187; 29...Nd8, 123.

Black's queen blocks out White's, enabling the b-pawn to run. I could not consider exchanging on c4: That would straighten out Black's structure and leave the c-pawn too close to my first rank.

There were two main moves that I analyzed: **30 Qf5+** and **30 Qf8**.

After 30 Qf8, Bacrot was suggesting 30...Qe2, reaching the ending I mentioned above after 31 Bxf4 Bxf4 32 Qxf4 Qxh5. That was one satisfactory possibility for Black, but there was also 30...b4 31 h6 b3 32 Qf5+ e6 (32...Kc7? 33 h7 b2 34 Bxf4! winning a pawn) 33 Qf7+ Kc8, when, remarkably, White has no way to profit from Black's exposed king.

In view of these variations, I went for 30 Qf5+.

18TH AUGUST

CROATIA

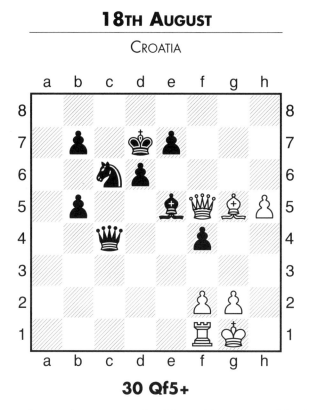

30 Qf5+

Black has only one decent move in this position. **30...e6** loses to 31 Qf7+ Kc8 32 h6 b4 33 h7, and White arrives first to queen; while **30...Kc7** is met spectacularly by 31 h6 Nd4 32 Qxe5! dxe5 33 h7 Ne2+ 34 Kh2 Ng3 35 Rg1! followed by queening on the next turn.

To a certain extent I think my move came as a surprise to the World Team. They had spent much of their time analyzing the position with queens on the board after 30 Qf8, but I had realized quite quickly that I would get nowhere without the support of the rook; so I turned my attention to the ending instead.

19TH AUGUST

CROATIA

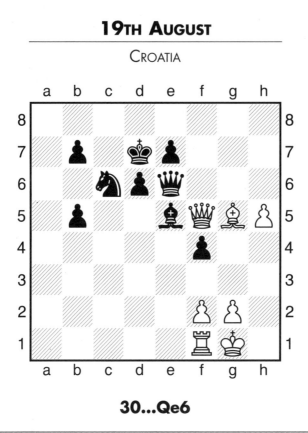

30...Qe6

Analysts' Recommendations: Krush, 30...Qe6; Paehtz, 30...Qe6; Felecan, 30...Qe6; Bacrot, no recommendation, as he was participating in the French national championship.

Voting Results: 30...Qe6, 5,760; 30...Kc7, 274; 30...e6, 262; 30...Ke8, 61; 30...Nd4, 40.

Blocking the check with the queen is absolutely forced.

Although the World Team was ahead of us in terms of analysis at the start of the game, by the time we had exchanged rooks on move 22, we had done a good job in regaining ground and were at least on level terms. I believe that 26...f4 was mainly an intuitive decision as there was not the usual mountain of analysis to justify it; so although we fell behind again at that point, we caught up quickly. Starting from 28 h4, we were ahead of them again in our understanding of the position.

At first, I was concerned that after **31 Qxe6+** Kxe6 32 g3 (so as to bring my rook into the game after the pawn exchanges), Black would close the position with 32...f3, with a very unclear situation. It would be difficult to bring my king across to the queenside to stop the b-pawn, for instance.

That's why I started investigating the possibility of **31 g4**. We had been analyzing the pawn move for several days with growing enthusiasm, particularly when we realized that the opposition was late in beginning a detailed study of the endgame. They would have little time to examine a highly treacherous position.

Black has two correct moves: 31...b4; and 31...fxg3. The latter transposes to the game after 32 Qxe6+ Kxe6 33 fxg3, but avoids the possibility of 32...f3—that is the point—though it turns out we had this one under control.

And there are two poor moves. 31...Qxf5 would be an error. The e-pawn would be neutralized, White's h-pawn would be ready to roll and, perhaps more important, the king would be able to come out to support it. For example:

31 g4 Qxf5? 32 gxf5 Nd4 33 Kg2! Nxf5 34 Kf3! b4 35 Rb1 Bc3 36 Kxf4 e6 37 Ke4 d5+ 38 Kd3, and the ending is very pleasant for White, possibly winning, e.g. 38...e5 39 f3 Nd4 40 Bd2 Bxd2 41 Kxd2 Nxf3+ 42 Ke3 Ng5 43 h6, and with the help of the rook, the h-pawn touches down.

Likewise, 31...Nd4 is a mistake. White targets the knight:

31 g4 Nd4? 32 Qxe6+ Kxe6 33 Kg2 b4 34 Rd1! Kd5 (34 ...f3+ 35 Kh3 b3 36 Rb1 Kd5 37 Be3 Kc4 38 Bxd4 Bxd4 39 g5 wins) 35 Bxe7 b3 36 g5 Ke6 37 Bf6. Once the wonderful bishop in the middle is exchanged, Black is in trouble.

31...b4 is the best move:

31 g4 b4! 32 Rb1! Eventually, the rook will have to sacrifice itself, but in the meantime it can slow the pawn's progress down the board. 32...Nd4 33 Qxe6+ Kxe6 34 Bh6 (34 Rxb4? Nf3+) 34...b3 35 Kg2 Kd5! The king

hastens to support the b-pawn. And White advances on the other side of the board. 36 g5 Kc4.

The position is so double-edged that one false move, for either side, could prove fatal. For instance, if I play the seemingly natural 37 g6, then Black wins: 37 ..Nf5! 38 Bf8 Kc3 39 Kf3 Kc2 40 Rg1 b2 41 Ke4 e6 42 h6 Bd4! (avoiding 42 ..b1Q? 43 Rxb1 Kxb1 44 Bxd6! saving White) 43 h7 (43 g7 d5+ 44 Kxf4 Nxh6 wins) 43 ..Bxf2! 44 g7 Bxg1 45 g8Q b1Q 46 h8Q. A position that has more in common with the problem composer Genrikh Kasparian than Garry Kasparov! There is more than one way for Black to win, but 46...Qf1! threatening, among others, ...Qe2+, is my favorite.

Instead, 37 Bf8 is the correct move. My original idea when examining this variation was 37...Kc3 38 h6 Nf5 39 Kf3 Kc2? 40 Rxb3! Kxb3 41 Ke4 e6 42 Bxd6! Bc3 43 Be5 Nh4 44 Bxc3 Kxc3 45 Ke5 winning; but Black can improve on this.

Instead of 39...Kc2? the correct idea is 39...e6! so that after 40 Ke4, Black avoids the sacrifice on d6 with 40...Bd4! White has nothing better than to head for a draw with 41 Rxb3+ Kxb3 42 Bxd6 Bxf2 43 Be5 Ne7 44 h7 Ng6 45 h8Q Nxh8 46 Bxh8 Bc5 47 g6 Bf8 48 Kxf4 Kc4 49 Ke5 b5 50 Kxe6 b4 51 Kf7 Bh6. The b-pawn prevents any winning attempt by White.

This is certainly not the only way for Black to draw. I began to realize that in these variations Black could not only survive, but even trick me if I wasn't careful. 31 g4 was just too risky to play. It was a pity, because there are some unbelievable tactics in these variations, but, objectively, it was the correct decision on my part. In the good old days of adjournments, these kinds of lines could have been considered. With a limited period of time to analyze, one's opponent could easily make a blunder, or simply an error of judgement. But one could not compare this game with an old-fashioned adjournment. With our slow-motion struggle, my opponents would have found the correct solution days in advance.

20TH AUGUST

CROATIA

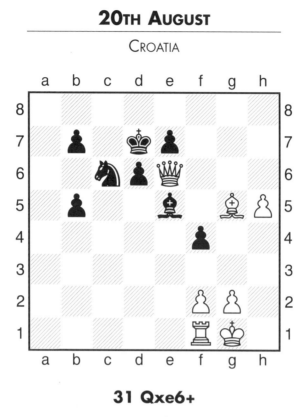

31 Qxe6+

I had to employ my common sense. Exchanging queens would help me to activate the rook.

21ST AUGUST

CROATIA

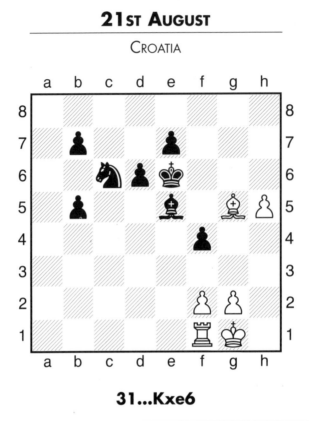

31...Kxe6

Analysts' Recommendations: Krush, 31...Kxe6; Paehtz, 31...Kxe6; Florin Felecan, no recommendation; Bacrot, no recommendation, as he was participating in the French national championship.

Voting Results: 31...Kxe6, 5,646; 31...Ke8, 37; 31...Kc7, 31; 31...Kd8, 13; 31...Nd8, 7.

The World Team had not analyzed this endgame in too much detail, assuming that Black's position was quite satisfactory. In that respect they were right. With active and well-protected minor pieces, and a centralized king ready to block the passed h-pawn or support its own passed b-pawn, Black should be fine. However, they were perhaps mistaken in not looking at the finer details of the position because, with my next move, I almost wiped them out.

We had more or less anticipated the sequence of moves since I declined the draw with 28 h4. Apart from considering 31 g4, there had not been any major decisions, so when I arrived at this position, I had known for some time exactly what my next move would be. Endgames are mainly about pushing passed pawns toward the eighth rank to get a new queen. I have a valuable passed h-pawn, but it would be nothing without the support of the rest of White's army. I also had to think about how I was going to prevent the advance of Black's b-pawn.

It was clear that my objectives remained the same: to activate the bishop and rook, and my next move went some way toward achieving these goals.

22ND AUGUST

CROATIA TO BESANCON

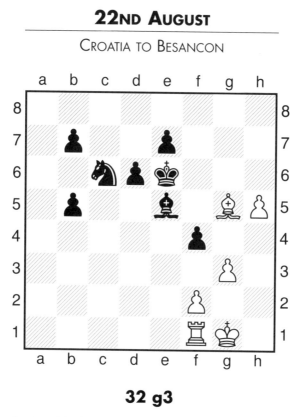

32 g3

Ever since the World played 10...Qe6, Black's pieces had been far more active than mine. 32 g3 was my attempt to cut the Gordian knot. With the sacrifice of just one pawn, I could reconnect my bishop with the other side of the board; activate my rook on f1; and even open the way for my king to enter the game.

I knew that if Black captured the pawn, I would not, at the very least, have problems. As I mentioned previously, the move that initially concerned me was **32...f3**, keeping the position as closed as possible, and that was what we mainly analyzed before playing 32 g3. Once again, the variations are so complex that it is difficult to give a definitive assessment. However, it is possible to say that White would be in no danger at all, and there would be chances to play for a win. Considering what I had been through earlier in the game, that was quite enough to satisfy me.

32...f3 is an ambitious move, although not a terribly sound one. Black attempts to keep White's king and rook blocked in. It is vital that White activates the rook. Smart Chess mainly considered 33 Rb1, while we concentrated on 33 Rd1. It seems that both moves give White the better chances.

Here are the principal variations after 33 Rd1:

a. 33...Kf5 34 Bc1! b4 35 Rd3 Bc3! (35...Kg4 36 h6) 36 Rxf3+ Kg4 37 Rf8 Kxh5 38 Rg8 Nd4 (38...Bf6? 39 Kg2 Ne5 40 Kh3 b3 41 f3 wins) 39 Be3 Ne6 40 Kg2 Bd4 (40...b3? 41 g4+ Kh4 42 Rg6! Nf8 43 Rg5 Ne6 44 f3! and Black has been caught in a beautiful mating net) 41 Re8!

b. 33...Bc3?! 34 Rd3 Nd4 35 h6 Kf7 36 Bxe7 is good for White.

c. 33...Nd4?! 34 Rd3 Ne2+ 35 Kf1 Nc3 36 h6.

d. 33...b4 34 Rd3 Bc3 35 Re3+ Kf7! 36 Rxf3+ Kg8, and now two options:

   i. 37 Rd3 Ne5 38 Re3 is unclear (38 Rd5? b3 39 Rb5 b2 40 Bxe7 Nc6 wins).

   ii. 37 Kf1 Nd4 38 Rd3 b3 39 Rd1 (39 Rxc3 b2 40 Rc1 bxc1Q+ 41 Bxc1) 39...b2 40 Rb1 Nc2 41 Bc1 Na3 42 Rxb2 Bxb2 43 Bxb2 Nc4. A draw is the most likely result here, but it is White who is pressing for the win.

Black could also consider leaving the f-pawn to its fate so as to gain time for advancing the b-pawn, but it doesn't help: It allows me to exchange the bishops—one of my core objectives:

32 ..b4? 33 Bxf4 Bxf4 34 gxf4 Kd5? The most critical move, supporting the b-pawn, but hopelessly slow: 35 h6 Nd8 36 h7 Nf7. What a difference without the Black bishop on e5—the knight is consigned to a humiliating defense. White finishes off with a perfect demonstration of why the rook is such an effective long-range piece: 37 Rb1! Kc4 . . . the king is dragged over . . . 38 Re1 . . . so now the e-pawn cannot be protected 38...b3 39 Rxe7 b2 40 Rxb7 Kc3 41 Kg2. Threat: take the knight and queen. 41...Nh8 42 Kf3 Kc2 43 Ke4. The rook gives itself for the b-pawn, then the f-pawn charges up the board supported by the king. Too much for the knight to cope with on its own.

This variation is not only a good illustration of the power of a rook on an open board but also how poor a knight can be under such conditions—it can only operate in one sector. On the other hand there are many variations in this game where a bishop is able to match the rook as it is also a long-range piece, able to operate on both sides of the board.

I left Croatia on August 22nd for Besancon, a small town near the French alps, where I was due to give a simultaneous exhibition. I flew to Geneva, met up with the French documentary film crew, then drove down with them across the border, arriving in the evening.

23RD AUGUST

BESANCON

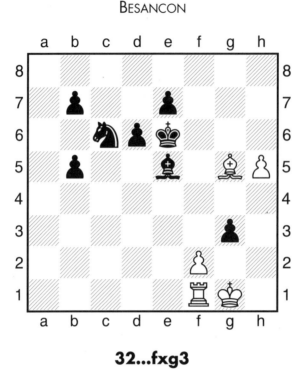

32...fxg3

Analysts' Recommendations: Krush, 32...fxg3; Paehtz, 32...f3; Felecan, 32...fxg3; Bacrot, no recommendation, as he was participating in the French national championship.

Voting Results: 32...fxg3, 3,718; 32...f3, 975; 32...Kf5, 194; 32...Nd4, 118; 32...b4, 51.

The World played the best move. But the question was: After I recaptured, would they capture a second time?

Simultaneous displays are physically and mentally demanding, and I take them very seriously—I feel it is my professional duty to do so. In other words, I try to win all the games, and I believe my opponents expect nothing less of me. If I happen to score a draw or a loss, then so be it; and in that case the players will have the satisfaction of knowing that I was giving my all.

The opposition in Besancon was not particularly strong, and after a couple of hours most of the games were turning in my favor; only three players were holding the balance. Then one of them offered me a draw. I believe that offering a draw in a simultaneous display is a Grandmaster's privilege. Now I was absolutely determined to go for a total wipe out. It took me a long time, four hours, but in the end I made it: 25-0.

The simultaneous was being played alongside the French national championship in which Etienne Bacrot was participating. It was curious to meet one of my analyst adversaries from the World Team, though it was clear that he wasn't busting his brain trying to beat me. We had time to exchange a few words, but nothing more. I was very tired and he was in the middle of a long match.

24TH AUGUST

GENEVA

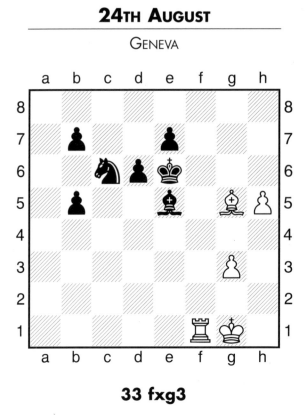

33 fxg3

Quite a transformation. For most of this game the rook on f1 has played no part in the proceedings, now it magically finds meaning to its existence: Black's king is prevented from marching across to block White's h-pawn.

Still, we established fairly quickly that **33...b4** 34 Bf4 Bh8 should be a draw. And then we saw the World Team devoting all their time to analyzing **33...Bxg3**. I was amazed. I don't know whether this was just the natural human instinct to grab a free lunch, or whether people were following their computer's suggestion. Perhaps my opponents were confused by the change in the situation on the board and were looking to escape with a forced draw.

Whatever the reason, even at a cursory glance one could see that with this option Black was treading close to defeat. If the World Team had invested 10 percent of the time they spent on 33...Bxg3 and instead, scrutinized 33...b4, they would have found the correct defense—34...Bh8.

To me this was a clear sign that my opponents were uncomfortable with their situation: The pawn grab is an attempt to force a draw, but nothing more. For the first time in the game, it felt as though I had taken control.

Still, it meant that, along with the World Team, we had to devote some time to looking at the capture, too. The main line runs:

33...Bxg3 34 h6 Be5 35 h7.

(In the time it took to take one single pawn and return again, I have managed to advance a pawn to within one step of transforming to a queen and instant victory. It cannot be right for Black to play like this. Here many players were seriously considering 35...Bg7 36 Rf8 b4 37 h8Q Bxh8 38 Rxh8 b3 39 Kf2, when Black has chances to construct a fortress with knight and four pawns against rook and bishop; but I don't believe it is good enough. Frankly, I did not even consider this possibility in any depth. If it happened, then we would analyze it. For me it was just important to see that I was playing for the win.)

35...Bh8 36 Rf8 Ne5! 37 Rxh8 Nf3+ 38 Kf2 Nxg5.

(For the moment, Black's knight prevents White from moving the rook, so the king must be brought into battle. Black can never play ...Kf7, as Rf8+ wins immediately.)

39 Ke3 b4 40 Kf4.

(The knight cannot move away from attacking the h-pawn, and 40...Nxh7 41 Rxh7 is a simple win for the rook as White's king is already active.)

40...b3 41 Kxg5 b2 42 Rf8!

(The best square when it comes to shielding the White king from checks.)

42 ..b1Q 43 h8Q.

(Queen and rook against queen is normally enough to force a win, but here White's king has to find a way to escape the checks from the queen. It requires delicate footwork, but it can be done. I discovered how to avoid the perpetual while thinking about the position on the way to the airport in Croatia.)

43...Qg1+ 44 Kf4 Qf2+ 45 Ke4 Qe2+ 46 Kd4 Qd2+ 47 Kc4 d5+ 48 Kb3 Qd1+ 49 Ka2 Qc2+ 50 Qb2 Qa4+ 51 Kb1 Qd1+ 52 Qc1 Qb3+ 53 Ka1 Qa4+ 54 Kb2 Qb4+ 55 Kc2 Qc4+ 56 Kd2 Qd4+ 57 Ke2 Qg4+ 58 Rf3 Qg2+ 59 Rf2 Qg4+ 60 Kd3 Qe4+ 61 Kd2 Qd4+ 62 Ke1 Qb4+ 63 Kf1 Qb5+ 64 Kg2. Black has no more checks, so now my queen and rook will get to work.

It took us some time to find out how to win this position with rook and queen against queen. It is a rather intriguing geometrical escape. The problem was that someone on the World Team found it, too: There were too many of them analyzing!

It is curious. The people who were behind such aggressive moves as sacrificing the exchange, and 18...f5, and 26...f4, would never consider a move such as 33...Bxg3. It was as though the leader had disappeared for a while. However, in the end, reason caught up with them and they returned to 33...b4.

25TH AUGUST

MOSCOW

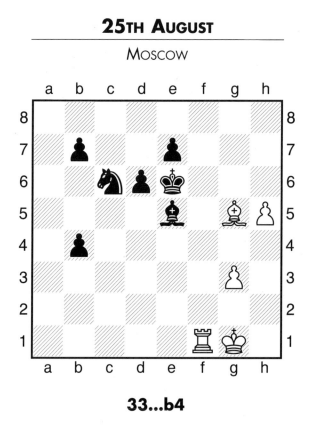

33...b4

The World correctly advanced the passed b-pawn, setting up some much-needed counter play on the queenside. My opponents were now anticipating that I would play **34 Kf2**, bringing the king over to block the b-pawn. However, in that case it shouldn't be too difficult for Black to hold the draw. As ever, there are many possible continuations for both sides, but the following are representative variations:

34...b3 and now two main possibilities:

a. 35 Bd2 Kd5 36 g4 Ke4 37 g5 Kd3 38 Be3 b2 (thanks to the active king, Black is going to be able to win the rook for the b-pawn. But before that happens, White's pawns on the kingside must be halted or eliminated) 39 h6 Nd8! (so as to cover the g7 square) 40 g6 Ne6 41 Kf3 (instead 41 g7 Nxg7! 42 hxg7 Bxg7, then after the rook is won for the b-pawn it is Black who has the winning chances!) 41...Kc2 42 Ke4 b1Q 43 Rxb1 Kxb1 44 Kf5 Ng7+ 45 hxg7 Bxg7 46 Ke6 b5 47 Bg5. White can take the e- and d-pawns, reaching a draw.

b. 35 Bf4 Bh8! 36 g4 Nb4 37 g5 b2 38 g6 Nc2 39 h6 Na3 40 Re1+ Kf6 41 g7 Bxg7 42 hxg7 Kf7 43 Rxe7+ Kxe7 44 g8Q b1Q 45 Qg7+ with a draw. This time, instead of the king, Black uses the knight to force the b-pawn through, then the king takes care of the kingside pawns with the bishop.

26TH AUGUST

MOSCOW

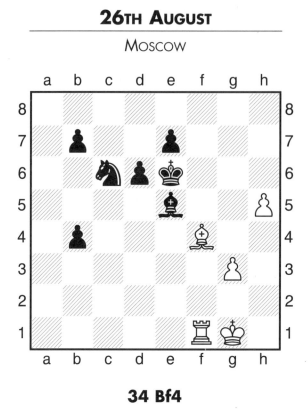

34 Bf4

It seems that my opponents had hardly considered this rather natural move, offering an exchange of bishops, and at the same time clearing the path for the g-pawn to advance. After 34 Bf4, there was some confusion on the bulletin boards. Some people accused Irina Krush of not seeing the move. I don't know where the "steady hand" was who had been guiding the World's play earlier, or perhaps I do: Khalifman was still in Las Vegas.

When we saw our opponents wasting time analyzing the wrong continuation, Yuri got very excited, "Garry, maybe we have a chance!"

I said, "C'mon Yuri, it is a draw. They just play ...Bh8..."

"But if they don't...?"

The draw we had found went:

34...Bh8! 35 g4 b3 36 g5 b2 37 g6. (The pawns look terrifying, but Black has sufficient counter play) 37...Nd4! (The d4 square belongs to the knight, not the bishop!) 38 h6 Ne2+ 39 Kh1 b1Q 40 Rxb1 Nxf4 41 g7 (41

Rg1 Nxg6 42 Rxg6+ Kf7 is a drawn position) 41...Bxg7 42 hxg7 Kf7 43 Rxb7 Ng6, followed by Kxg7. Knight and two pawns against a rook is a known theoretical draw.

Whether the World went in for this or not, we had, at the very least, created a little disturbance in the enemy camp and, having been on the receiving end of so many surprises in this game, it felt good.

27TH AUGUST

MOSCOW

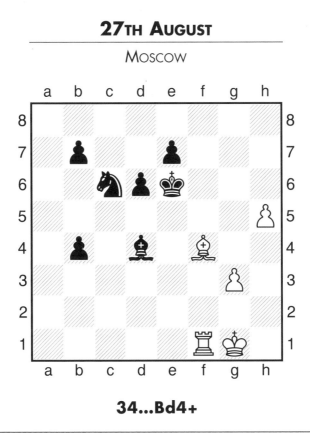

34...Bd4+

Analysts' Recommendations: Krush, 34...Bd4+; Paehtz, 34...Bd4+; Felecan, 34...Bd4+; Bacrot, no recommendation, as he was participating in the French national championship.

Voting Results: 34...Bd4+, 5556; 34...Bxf4, 210; 34...b3, 200; 34...Nd4, 103; 34...Bf6, 95.

Even though the World hardly considered the best move, 34...Bh8, by now it was clear to us that after 34...Bd4+ **35 Kg2** Black would still be able to hold the draw. The players in St. Petersburg knew it, too. Here is the main variation:

35 Kg2 b3 36 g4 Nb4 37 Kf3 b2 38 Ke2 Kd5 39 h6 Na2 40 Kd3 Nb4+! (a key move) 41 Kd2 (a risky attempt to play for a win; 41 Ke2 Na2 is a draw) 41...Kc4 42 g5 Bc3+ 43 Ke2 Nc2 44 g6 Nd4+ 45 Ke3 Nf5+ 46 Ke2 d5 (46...Nd4+ is a draw straightaway) 47 Kb1 d4 48 g7 d3+ 49 Kd1 Nxg7 50 Bd2 Bd4 51 Be3 Bf6 52 Bg5. A nice way to force a draw; Black's bishop must keep protecting the knight on g7, so White's bishop follows it eternally to force a draw.

To be honest, after 34...Bd4+, I thought the game was going to end in a draw. I just couldn't find a way to create any real difficulties for Black.

It was just a few days before I was due to go to London for a press conference to promote the game to European Internet audiences. I had lunch at home. Yuri was there because we were going to check some of our opening preparation in the afternoon. During lunch, Yuri said, "What if we play Kh1?"

It took me one minute to get the point—after Nb4, Nd3 there is no check—but still, I said, "Yuri, come on, you cannot be serious. . . !" The idea of putting the king in the corner of the board, when in the ending it should really be heading into the middle, seemed too outlandish. Yet it was strong.

I called Boris. He was ecstatic. At first he didn't dare to believe it— "Impossible!" he said—but he quickly appreciated the strength of the idea. Forget the opening preparation. We spent six hours analyzing the position after **35 Kh1**, three brains with three machines running simultaneously: my desktop computer at home, another lap-top, and Deep Junior in Tel Aviv. For a moment we thought we were winning. We couldn't find a defense. Pushing the b-pawn was losing; Nb4 was losing; this was losing, that was losing. Our confidence was growing.

Then just before Yuri left that evening, something occurred to me: "What about ...Ne5 and ...dxe5...?" Not good. We had found a clear draw for our opponents. Nevertheless, 35 Kh1 had to be tried. It was definitely the best chance in the position, particularly when it was going to come as a complete surprise. And besides that, finding 35 Kh1 filled us with confidence. It motivated us to carry on the struggle. Up to this point, I didn't feel as though I had played remarkably. It was my opponents who had been mainly dictating events. After this extraordinary move, I felt as though I deserved victory.

28TH AUGUST

MOSCOW

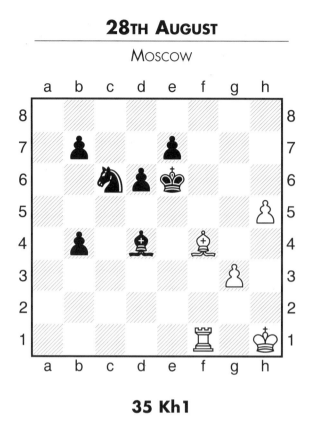

35 Kh1

There was total panic on the bulletin boards. No one had anticipated Kh1. On the Smart Chess site they even published a disclaimer saying they accepted no responsibility for the correctness of their analysis or the result of the game. The St. Petersburg crowd quickly posted a short piece of analysis with the claim that Kh1 was a mistake—then they fell silent for two days. It must have dawned on them that they were in serious trouble.

Let's take a look at 35 Kh1 in more detail. The move is difficult to foresee, as it is counterintuitive: It runs against the accepted notion that the king should be used actively in the endgame. With fewer pieces on the board, the king is in little danger of being checkmated so it becomes a powerful piece. So why play it into the corner?

There is one crucial variation where it suits White to have the king on h1 rather than g2 or h2. First let me give you the whole variation: **35...b3** 36 g4 b2 37 g5 Nb4 38 g6 Nd3 39 h6 b1(Q) 40 Rxb1 Nxf4 41 Re1+ Be5 42 g7 Kf7 43 Rg1, with a winning position for White. Let's go back through that from the beginning.

Black keeps to the plan of advancing the b-pawn to the queening square: 35...b3. White answers with 36 g4, and Black pushes the pawn on again with 36...b2. White pushes on again, 37 g5. Black cannot get a queen immediately, as the rook covers the promotion square b1. So the knight is thrown in to assist: 37...Nb4. White pushes on again, 38 g6. Black moves the knight in with 38...Nd3, attacking the bishop, but, instead of moving the bishop, White can ignore the threat and pushes again with 39 h6.

Only at this point is it possible to see why the king must go into the corner. If Black wins the bishop according to the variation I gave above with 39...b1(Q) 40 Rxb1 Nxf4, because the king stands on h1, instead of g2, White is not in check, so therefore has a free move to force the pawns home, and this can be done with the clever 41 Re1+. Whichever way Black gets out of this check, he is lost. For instance, moving the king away to d7 is just too far from the White pawns; and 41...Kf6 loses to 42 g7 Kf7 43 Rxe7+. While 41...Be5, as I gave above, loses to 42 g7 Kf7 (the only way to prevent White queening); but now 43 Rg1 does the trick as 43...Kg8 loses to 44 h7+. This is the justification for moving the king into the corner. If the king were on g2, in the variation above Black would capture the bishop on f4 with check, losing one vital move for White.

You might well ask, "Wouldn't it do just as well for the king to be on h2?" (indeed, Florin Felecan suggested this in his analysis). Here's the critical variation with the refutation: 35 Kh1 b3 36 g4, and now, instead of 36...b2 as I gave above, Black could try 36...Nb4, and if 37 g5 Nd3. The knight arrives a move earlier, but White ignores it: 38 h6 Nxf4 39 Rxf4 b2 40 Rf1, and Black has no decent defense against the advance of White's pawns, supported by the king. The point is that if White's king had been on h2, then Black could have played 39...Be5, pinning the rook to the king, and winning. Nevertheless, Florin was certainly on the right lines when he was looking for a square that avoided a check on f4.

Yet there was still a draw to be found: **35...Ne5** 36 Bxe5 dxe5! There is no escaping from the conclusion that chess is a fundamentally logical game. Although there are sound reasons for playing the White king to h1—as we saw in the variations above—there is a disadvantage, too: It is far from the center, which this recapture exploits. In this case it would suit White to have the king blockading the pawn on the e-file.

Recapturing with the d-pawn was the paradoxical idea I had hit upon the day before. It looks ugly to double the pawns like this, but there is a good reason for it. When the e-pawn reaches e2 it attacks the rook, forcing it to move from its excellent position on f1. Once the rook is disturbed, the Black king will be able to move across to blockade the White pawns. In addition, the e-pawn queens on a Black square, so given a chance, the bishop can assist in forcing it home. White can attempt to break down the defense in a variety of ways, but the most challenging is obviously the immediate advance of the g- and h-pawns:

37 g4 b3 38 h6 e4 39 g5 e3 40 g6 e2 41 Re1 b2 42 Kg2 Bc3! (42...Kf6? doesn't quite work: 43 g7 Kf7 44 Kf3 Bc3 45 Rg1 e1N+ 46 Ke2 Bxg7 47 hxg7 wins) 43 Rxe2+ Kf6 44 g7 b1Q, and Black draws: 45 Rf2+ (45 g8Q Qg6+ 46 Qxg6+ Kxg6 is even simpler as the h-pawn drops) 45...Ke5 46 g8Q Qe4+ 47 Kh3 Qh1+ 48 Rh2 Qf1+ 49 Qg2 Qf5+ 50 Qg4 Qf1+ with perpetual check.

In any event, at this time our opponents gave **35...b3** the most consideration, and for the first time in the game we could sense that they were struggling. The hunt was on. The more chances we discovered, the more excited and determined we became to win the game. We drove each other on in our analysis. It was actually Yuri who was the most vigorous of the three of us. In a strange way, he was upset: Our training sessions in Croatia had been ruined, and our World Team opponents were going to have to pay for it.

29TH AUGUST

LONDON

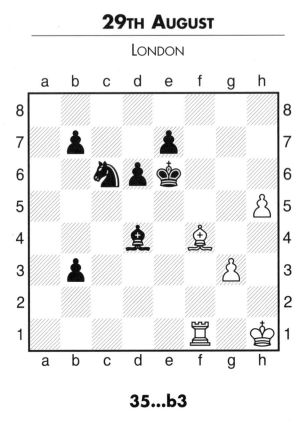

35...b3

Analysts' Recommendations: Krush, 35...b3; Paehtz, 35...b3; Felecan, 35...b3; Bacrot, 35...b3.

Voting Results: 35... b3, 3,586; 35...Ne5, 115; 35...Kf5, 74; 35...Kd5, 30; 35...Nd8, 28.

By the time I arrived in London, the analysis was already quite deep. We believed that 36 g4 Kd5 37 g5 e6 would lose for Black, so we concentrated our efforts on cracking 37...e5.

30TH AUGUST

LONDON

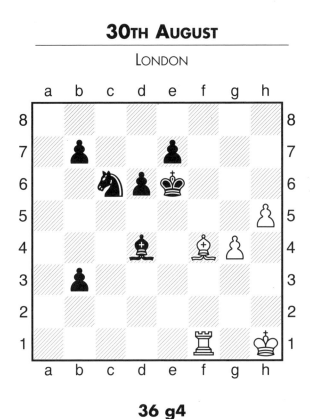

36 g4

It was clear that I had to push my g-pawn. Now Black has to vary from the line I gave above: **36...b2** 37 g5 Nb4 38 g6 Nd3 39 h6 b1(Q) 40 Rxb1 Nxf4 41 Re1+ Be5 42 g7 Kf7 43 Rg1 wins for White. There is a bewildering range of options: **36...Kd7**; **36...Nd8**; **36...Nb4**; **36...Kf7**; **36...Ne5**; **36...Bc3**; and even **36...Bh8**, admitting that 34...Bd4+ was a wasted move, but difficult to beat all the same.

31ST AUGUST

LONDON

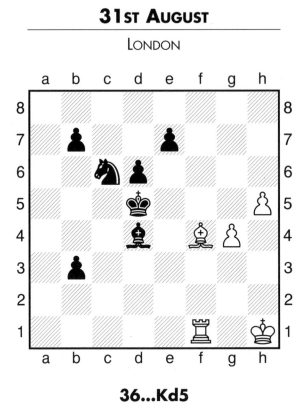

36...Kd5

Analysts' Recommendations: Krush, 36...Kd5; Paehtz, 36...Nb4;
Felecan, 36...b2; Bacrot, 36...b2.

Voting Results: 36...Kd5, 1,755; 36...b2, 1,728; 36...Nb4, 668;
36...Ne5, 168; 36...Kf6, 51.

The World Team was like a flock without a leader. They were just a
handful of votes away from choosing 36...b2, a move that they probably
knew was tantamount to resignation.

Instead, this king move narrowly won the vote. As well as striding over
to support the b-pawn, the king makes room for the e-pawn, which in turn
makes room for the knight to retreat to e7 to slow up the g- and h-pawns.
It looks laborious but, as we were to discover, it was actually strong enough
to hold the game.

1st September

London

37 g5

It was the night before the press conference, and I was to meet the Microsoft representatives to finalize details for the morning. Yuri, Boris and I were still working fiercely on the nuances of the position; and just before dinner we found an extraordinary win. I thought the game was in the bag. The main line runs:

37...e5 38 Bc1 Ne7 39 Rf7 Ke6 40 Rf6+ Kd7 41 Ba3 b5 42 Rxd6+ Ke8 43 h6 b2 44 Bxb2 Bxb2 45 g6 e4 46 Ra6 e3 47 Kg2 Nf5 48 h7 e2 49 Kf2 Bg7 50 Ra7 Ne7 51 Ra8+ Kd7 52 Rg8, and one of the pawns goes through.

Let's go through it again, this time filling in the details:

37...e5 38 Bc1 Ne7.

The knight has to retreat to halt the pawns. Instead 38...b2 39 Bxb2 Bxb2 is too casual. The neatest variation is 40 h6 e4 41 g6 e3 42 g7 Ne7 43 Rf7 Ng8 44 h7 e2 45 hxg8Q e1Q+ 46 Rf1+, winning with a discovered check.

39 Rf7

White does best to hit the knight immediately. 39 g6 is too slow:
39...b2 40 Bxb2 Bxb2 41 g7 Ng8 42 Rf8 Nh6 43 g8Q+ Nxg8 44 Rxg8 e4
45 Kg2 b5 46 Kf1 b4 47 h6 b3 48 h7 Bd4 49 h8Q Bxh8 50 Rxh8 Kc4 is
good enough to draw.

39...Ke6

Absolutely forced. The knight cannot afford to move away, e.g. 39...Ng8
40 Rg7 traps it.

40 Rf6+ Kd7

The king cannot return: 40...Kd5 41 h6 e4 42 h7 Bxf6 43 gxf6 Ng6 44
f7, and one of the pawns goes through. After 40...Kd7, White cannot
attempt the same idea, as in this final position Black's king could just nudge
to e7 to stop the f-pawn.

41 Ba3! b5!

A very tricky move. Black hopes to deflect the bishop away from b2 by
sacrificing the second b-pawn.

42 Rxd6+ Ke8

The king must stay as close to the kingside pawns as possible.

43 h6 b2

(43...b4? 44 h7 wins)

44 Bxb2 Bxb2 45 g6 e4 46 Ra6!!

I had actually given up on this variation, believing it to be drawn. It was
Yuri's persistence that found this beautiful winning move.

White threatens Ra8+ Kf7, Ra7+ Ke6, then g7 and Rxe7. This is the
move that took us so long to discover. With those two plump White pawns
on the sixth rank getting closer to promotion, one would imagine there
would be an easy win, but this is the only way we found. Black is often able
to save the game in the most remarkable way. The most direct move, 46 g7,
runs into 46...Bxg7 47 hxg7 Ng8! followed by ...Kf7 and draws.

46 Re6 is trickier: 46...Kd7 47 Ra6 Bd4 48 Kg2 b4 49 g7 b3 50 Ra4
Bxg7 51 hxg7 b2 52 Rb4 Ke6 53 Rxb2 Kf6 54 Rb7 Ng8 55 Kf2 Nh6! 56
Ke2 Kg6. White cannot make further progress as 57 Ke3 is met by ...Nf5+,

winning the last pawn and securing a drawn position. It is worth comparing this position to the famous game between Emanuel Lasker and Edward Lasker from the New York tournament in 1924. The World Champion drew a similar ending with just a king and knight against king, rook and pawn. In that case, Black's pawn was on the sixth rank, again, securely blockaded by the knight; and the king was also unable to approach to break down the defense.

And why doesn't 46 Rb6 work as well as 46 Ra6? Because it is on the wrong-colored square: 46 Rb6 e3 47 Kg2 e2. This time, White cannot play 48 Kf2 because of 48...Bd4+. So the rook must return, and then Black seizes the chance to attack the pawns. 48 Re6 Kf8 49 Rxe2 Bc1 50 Rf2+ Ke8 51 h7 Nxg6, and draws.

46...e3.

Instead, if 46...Bd4, preventing the rook moving to a7, 47 Re6! wins. This time it works as 47...Kd7 is met by 48 Rxe4, gaining a tempo on the bishop.

47 Kg2

White has to take care of the e-pawn before advancing the pawns.

47...Nf5 48 h7 e2 49 Kf2 Bg7 50 Ra7 Ne7 51 Ra8+ Kd7 52 Rg8. Once the bishop moves, 53 g7 forces one of the pawns home.

The timing was perfect. For me, that evening at the wonderful La Tante Claire restaurant in Knightsbridge felt like a celebration party. Eddie Ranchigoda and Diane McDade, the Microsoft management team from Seattle, were there; people from the PR firm in London; Danny King, who would be hosting the press conference; and my agent, Owen Williams. I was confident enough in our analysis to announce to the table that the game would, in all likelihood, be over in two weeks. And in the morning I would announce it to the World.

2ND SEPTEMBER

LONDON

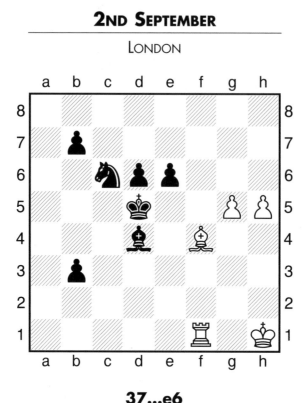

37...e6

> **Analysts' Recommendations:** Krush, 37...e6; Paehtz, 37...e5; Felecan, 37...e6; Bacrot, 37...e6.
>
> **Voting Results:** 37...e6, 3,407; 37...e5, 2,213; 37...b2, 262; 37...Nd8, 89; 37...Nb4, 53.

Boris woke at 7 AM in Tel Aviv. Deep Junior had been running overnight, checking a position he and Yuri had been discussing the night before. It had bad news. Boris called Yuri in Moscow, who then woke me at 9 AM London time, barely an hour before the press conference. Yuri said, "Garry, ...e6 is a draw. We can't see anything, we can't see a win after ...e6."

This was the line they had been researching. Black has to find a whole string of exact moves, but I felt that, with enough time, my opponents would find the correct way to draw. Once again, it is fantastically complicated, and I just present the main variations:

38 Rd1 Ke4! 39 Bxd6 Kf5 40 g6 Bg7! 41 Rg1 b5! 42 Ba3 b4 43 Bc1 b2. And now three main possibilities:

a. 44 Be3 Ke4 45 h6 Kxe3 46 hxg7 Ne7 47 Rb1 Kd2 (47...Ke4 also draws: 48 Rxb2 Kf5 49 Rxb4 Kxg6 50 Rg4+ Kf7, followed by ...Kg8 and ...Nf5) 48 Rxb2+ Kc3 49 Re2 b3 50 Rxe6 b2 51 Rb6 Kc2 52 Kg2 b1Q 53 Rxb1 Kxb1 54 Kf3 Kc2 55 Ke4 Ng8 56 Kf5 Kd3 57 Ke6 Ke4 58 Kf7 Nh6+ 59 Kf8 Kf5. Black's king arrives back just in time to draw.

b. 44 Bxb2 Bxb2 45 g7 Bxg7 46 Rxg7 b3 47 Rg2 Nd4 48 h6 b2 49 Rxb2 Kg6 50 Rh2 Kh7, followed by ...Nf5 and Nxh6, draws.

c. 44 Bd2 (White threatens Rf1 and h6, but) 44...Ne7!! (the only move) 45 Rf1 (45 Bxb4 Nd5 46 Ba3 Nf4 draws) 45...Ke4 46 h6 Kd3!! 47 Bxb4 Nf5!! 48 Rd1+ Kc2 49 hxg6 Kxd1 draws.

Instead of announcing my victory at the press conference, I went into it not knowing for certain whether I could win or whether the position really was drawn—I had no time to check the variations. When asked for my assessment of the position, I had to be cagey with my answers, as I really didn't know how the game would develop.

After the press conference was over, Boris, Yuri and I spent the whole day trying to break Black's defense. I knew I had the reserve option of a queen ending where I had the slightly better chances, but I wanted something clearer. However, by the time evening came I still hadn't found what I was looking for.

Around midnight I met up with Eddie. "I have bad news for you. We are about to head for an ending that could still be going at Christmas."

Eddie said, "What about my vacation to Sri Lanka?"

I replied, 'Sorry, but unless you introduce the multiple move option, this game could run and run. I don't see an end in sight."

Microsoft had been delighted by the response to the game, and was pleased that it had turned into such a tense and lengthy encounter. It had not been anticipated that the game would last beyond the end of August, but to Microsoft this was a bonus: The initial start-up costs of the project were considerable, but as the operation was mostly run in-house, the continuing costs were comparatively small; and the longer the game went on, the more traffic and awareness it generated for the MSN portal. Having said that, the prospect of the game going on into the new year did not appeal to Microsoft. The human resources devoted to the game were needed elsewhere. Therefore, the multiple move voting option came back on.

Back at the game, Smart Chess was preparing everyone for the worst. Irina wrote on the game site, "Alas, overnight analysis sessions suggest Black will have severe difficulties . . ." But five or six hours later, they had more or less found the right idea to save the game. Once again, they had discovered the correct defense. Although they had correctly rejected 37...e5 in favor of 37...e6, they had done so for the wrong reasons. Was this luck or keen intuition? It was probably a little of both.

In view of these discoveries, over the next twenty-four hours, it became clear to me that the queen ending was my only chance to play for a win.

3RD SEPTEMBER

LONDON TO MONACO

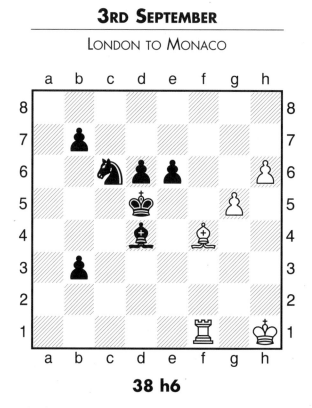

38 h6

Unfortunately for me, the pawns can be blockaded by the knight. This last move really commits me to playing into a queen ending.

From London I flew to Monaco to meet one of the chess world's most generous benefactors. Joop van Oosterom is a Dutchman who made a fortune in the software industry. He regularly sponsors tournaments, but unusually, he does not seek any kind of publicity in return for his financial support. He funds events purely out of his passion for chess. He has a good understanding of the game—he became an International Master at correspondence chess—but was always strictly an amateur.

Van Oosterom's tournaments often have unusual formats. For instance, he has held a whole series of "women versus veterans" events. He has also provided match practice for one of Holland's best players, Jeroen Piket; but the jewel in his crown is the Melody Amber tournament, named after his daughter, held annually in the luxurious setting of Monaco. Participants must play two forms of chess: rapid play, and blindfold. To this tournament, he regularly attracts the elite of the chess world, and it is a fine event, though I have to say I have never taken part. I do not play blindfold chess—it is simple as that. It is a very tiring discipline, and I do not believe it is worth expending so much energy on a form of chess that, apart from in the tournament itself, would not be beneficial to me in any other way.

Sadly, van Oosterom has recently had a stroke, impairing his speech, but his mind is obviously still as sharp as before. I showed him my game against the World, which he greatly enjoyed. On his part he was still trying to persuade me to play in the Melody Amber tournament, but I had to decline again.

4TH SEPTEMBER

MONACO TO ROTTERDAM

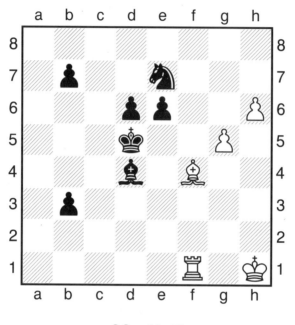

38...Ne7

Analysts' Recommendations: Krush, 38...Ne7; Paehtz, 38...Ne7; Felecan, 38...Ne7; Bacrot, 38...Ne7.

Voting Results: 38...Ne7, 5,230;   38...e5, 227;   38...b2, 125; 38...Ne5, 61; 38...Nb4, 18.

White cannot be allowed to play g6, so the knight must swing over to blockade the pawns.

My flight from Nice to Rotterdam was delayed for four hours. I spent most of that time on the phone to Boris in Israel discussing the possible queen ending with my pawn on h7—(see later on!)

Arriving in Rotterdam I found myself staying in the most bizarre place: the Hotel New York. This building was formerly the emigration station for those wishing to cross the Atlantic to start a new life in the USA—the last stop before Ellis Island. Memorabilia from the nineteenth century has been included in the new design: old trunks and packing cases, for example. Frankly, I found it all rather creepy. It was as though I could sense the spirits of those émigrés from the past, and it did nothing to help my mood for the next day.

5TH SEPTEMBER

ROTTERDAM

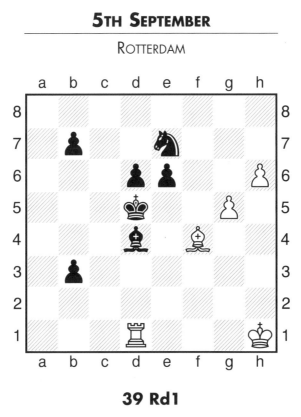

39 Rd1

On the face of it, quite an unpleasant move for Black to deal with. The pride of Black's position, the bishop, is pinned to the king; and there is a threat to play Bxd6, winning a pawn. For instance, **39...b2**, would now be a mistake: 40 Bxd6! b1(Q) 41 Rxb1 Kxd6 42 Rxb7 gives White excellent winning chances. While Black is tied up, White can slowly advance the king to support the pawns.

However, Black is able to defend after 39 Rd1.

I was in Rotterdam to play an exhibition game against Jan Timman as part of the Wereld Haven Festival. It was quite a spectacle. The event took place on the Maasvlakte, an artificial island in the North Sea for super-tankers. We played a normal rapid game in the office of the sponsor, ECT (Europe Combined Terminals), but the moves were played out for spectators on a giant chessboard with freight containers for pieces. Every time one of us moved, huge cranes, twenty meters high, would swing into action to move the containers around the board. It would take a couple of minutes before each move was complete.

It was rather a strange time control—twenty-five minutes each, plus however long it took for the cranes to shift the containers (that was the strange part)—and I never properly settled. I played unevenly and Jan took control. I lost in fifty-seven moves. Late on in the game, when it seemed as though my situation was already hopeless, I even missed a miracle draw.

My mind was elsewhere. It was now emerging into the public domain that the sponsorship for my match with Anand had fallen through and, of course, I was still intensely involved in the Microsoft game, which was, quite literally, intruding on my thoughts. There was a bizarre moment in the middle of my game with Timman when my mobile phone rang—I had forgotten to switch it off.

"Garry Kimovich…" said the voice on the other end of the phone.

"Boris, I am playing Timman! Let's speak later." I replied.

Luckily I was away from the board at the time, so I was spared any embarrassment. It seemed as though I could not escape from the game with the World wherever I went and whatever I was doing.

6TH SEPTEMBER

ROTTERDAM TO TEL AVIV

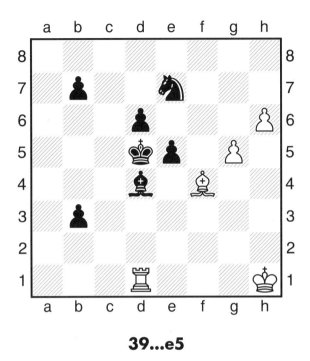

39...e5

> **Analysts' Recommendations:** Krush, 39...e5; Paehtz, 39...e5; Felecan, 39...e5; Bacrot, 39...e5.
>
> **Voting Results:** 39...e5, 4,493; 39...Ng6, 378; 39...b2, 262; 39...Nf5, 150; 39...Ke4, 87.

This is the best move, preventing the capture of the d-pawn and forcing me to lose a move as the bishop must be redeployed.

Instead of heading for the drawish queen ending with 40 Be3, I could have tried **40 Bc1**; a rather tricky attempt to play for a win. Yuri strongly advocated this move, but not entirely for its objective merit. He realized that in the queen ending Boris and Deep Junior would effectively take over the analysis of the game, while his role would diminish. Yet he still wanted to be involved in the fight, which he would be in the tricky, but more human, consequences of 40 Bc1. It is testament to his dedication and fighting spirit that Yuri took this line.

In fact the line Irina gave in her analysis after 40 Bc1 was losing—though I didn't realize it straightaway. Black's most straightforward continuation is to round up the two pawns on the kingside: 40...Ke6! 41 Ba3. It was here that Smart Chess was recommending 41...Bc5—a mistake. I had a brilliant riposte: 42 Rb1!! Bxa3 43 Rxb3 Bc1 44 h7 Ng6 45 Rxb7 e4 (45...Bxg5 46 Rg7 wins) 46 Rg7 Nh8 47 Rg8 Bb2 48 g6 e3 49 Kg2, and g7 cannot be stopped. It is interesting that computers just did not see this move, 42 Rb1. It came to me in my sleep: I woke up and it was in my mind, but that was after I had sent off my move **40 Be3**. I then spent the whole of the next day wondering whether I had missed a win—when I should have been giving my undivided attention to a simultaneous display.

Actually, we discovered that after 40 Bc1 Ke6 41 Ba3, Black can draw by playing 41...Kf5. White cannot protect the h- and g-pawns and at the same time control the b-pawn, so . . . 42 Rb1 Kxg5 43 h7 Ng6 44 Rxb3. Black only needs to eliminate White's last pawn and the game will be a draw. The easiest way to do that is to cause some confusion with the e-pawn: 44...e4! 45 Rxb7 e3 46 Kg2 e2 47 Bb4 Nh4+ 48 Kh3 Nf3 49 Rd7 e1Q 50 Bxe1 Nxe1 51 Rxd6 Bh8 52 Kg3 Nc2. White can win the bishop for the h-pawn but, with the knight escaping, the position is a theoretical draw. For once, it was a relief to discover that my opponents could hold the game.

7TH SEPTEMBER

TEL AVIV

40 Be3

Black needs to advance the b-pawn, but cannot do so immediately: 40...b2 41 Bxd4 exd4 42 Rb1 scoops it up. Therefore the king must come forward first, slipping out of the pin.

At last I was able to exchange off Black's superb bishop. Unfortunately, the benefits of the exchange were not as great as I had originally hoped. In fact, I was acquiescing to a queen ending where my opponents, while still having the worse position, would have excellent drawing chances.

At this moment, with a more or less forced sequence of moves ahead of us, I made another formal request that multiple move options be introduced. This time, with the prospect of the game heading into the new year, Microsoft was certainly more amenable to my suggestion. Eddie Ranchigoda promised to look into the feasibility of introducing the option with his technical team, and to consider any PR issues that might arise from the change.

On this day and the next I gave a rather unusual simultaneous exhibition. I sat in the headquarters of the Orange mobile phone company in front of a computer screen containing nine chess boards. My opponents were in another location, the Kasparov Chess Academy, relaying their moves to my computer screen via mobile phone. When one player lost, another took his or her place. In total I played eighty-four games over the two days—with a perfect score. But for much of that time I was seething over "missing" 40 Bc1 in the game against the World.

8TH SEPTEMBER

TEL AVIV

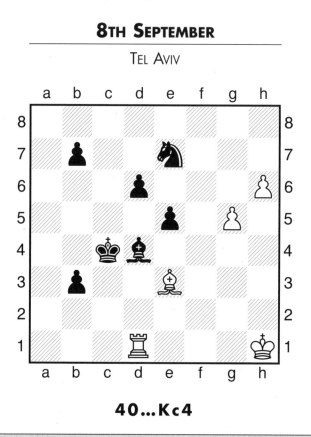

40...Kc4

Analysts' Recommendations: Krush, 40...Kc4; Paehtz, 40...Kc4; Felecan, 40...Kc4; Bacrot, 40...Kc4.

Voting Results: 40...Kc4, 5,106; 40...Ng6, 373; 40...Nf5, 278; 40...Ke4, 266; 40...b2, 215.

I have to carry through my plan to exchange bishops, so . . .

9TH SEPTEMBER

TEL AVIV

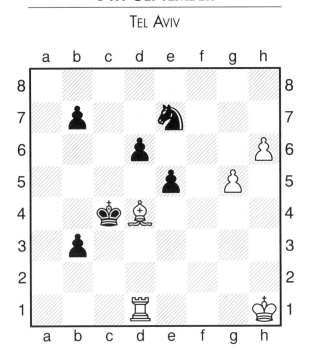

. . . and Black must recapture . . .

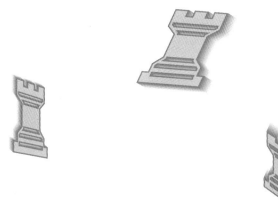

10TH SEPTEMBER

TEL AVIV

[Chess diagram showing position with Black pieces: pawns on b7, d6, c4(king on c4), d4, b3; knight on e7; White pieces: pawns on h6, g5; rook on d1; king on h1]

41...exd4

Analysts' Recommendations: Krush, 41...exd4; Paehtz, 41...exd4; Felecan, 41...exd4; Bacrot, 41...exd4.

Voting Results: 41...exd4, 6,521; 41...Ng6, 65; 41...e4, 28; 41...Nf5, 19; 41...b2, 13.

We are now in a situation where both sides must attempt to force their pawns through as quickly as possible. Black's knight holds up the kingside pawns, while my rook does the same on the other side of the board. I have to rush my king up the board to dislodge the knight and get my pawns rolling again, while Black's king is already in the perfect place, ready to support both the b- and d- pawns in their march to the eighth rank. The race was on, though the result was known to us all well in advance.

After consulting his team, Eddie Ranchigoda put forward a plan to implement multiple move options. I would be able to offer a sequence of moves, but it would only be voted on by the World if one of the analysts recommended it; moreover, any of the analysts could also offer a sequence of moves to be voted on. If the sequence won the vote, then the game would automatically jump ahead to the position at the end of the sequence. If the sequence did not win the vote, then my first move of the sequence would automatically be played. In order to avoid confusion, a limit of four move pairs was put on these move sequences. In other words, it was possible to save about a week at a stroke. The timings and implications were thought through carefully, necessary safeguards were put in place to ensure that no one was being rushed into a decision, and these conditions were clearly stated to all involved parties.

The proposal seemed fair to me. And to Etienne, Florin, Elisabeth and Danny. But not to Irina. It did not take long for a response to arrive from her, or perhaps I should say from her management team. It was unequivocal.

"If the rules of the game are changed while the game is in progress, I will tender my withdrawal from the event. The game would become null and void in my opinion."

She considered that the multiple move option ". . .would ultimately serve only to contribute to the destruction of the "greatest game of chess" ever played. The negative backlash and publicity would be permanent and insurmountable."

This was a prophecy that Irina's management team was perhaps intending to fulfill. The Microsoft executives were amazed by the strength of the reaction. The threat was clear. Eddie Ranchigoda asked Irina to reconsider her position. He received no response.

Smart Chess, Irina's management team, had a vested interest in creating as much publicity for her as possible, and in that respect her withdrawal from the game would be a wonderful opportunity for them. There was nothing to stop them holding their own press conference to publicize how they were supposedly wronged; and in such case, would anyone listen to Microsoft's viewpoint? Who would the press like to believe, a massive software corporation, or a pleading 15-year-old girl, who was being "robbed of the chance to complete the game of her life"?

After considering the situation for a few more days, Eddie decided to drop the whole idea: He could not risk having Irina withdraw from the event, and there was every chance that she would.

11TH SEPTEMBER

TEL AVIV

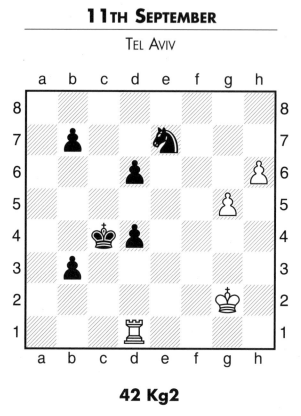

42 Kg2

With my rook busy preventing Black's pawns queening, I had no alternative but to advance my king to support my own pawns. Instead, checking with the rook on c1 would have brought no benefit at all.

In Tel Aviv, life was as hectic as usual. I spent most of my time around the Kasparov Chess Academy, discussing the setting up of Kasparov Chess Online; and a few days before this I had given a simultaneous display; and, of course, there was plenty of work to do with Boris and Deep Junior analyzing the World game. To add to all this, the French documentary film crew had followed me here to finish their filming.

12TH SEPTEMBER

TEL AVIV

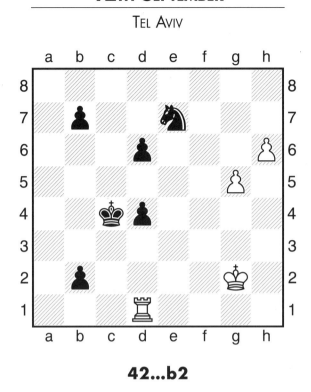

42...b2

> **Analysts' Recommendations:** Krush, 42...b2; Paehtz, 42...b2; Felecan, 42...b2; Bacrot, 42...b2.
>
> **Voting Results:** 42...b2, 3,510; 42...Ng6, 163; 42...c3, 136; 42...d3, 87; 42...Nf5, 41.

Now my rook really cannot move from the first rank; so it is onward and upward with the king.

13TH SEPTEMBER

TEL AVIV

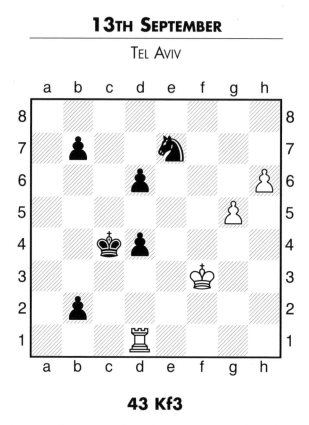

43 Kf3

Moving closer to the pawns, but also influencing the other side of the board.

14TH SEPTEMBER

TEL AVIV

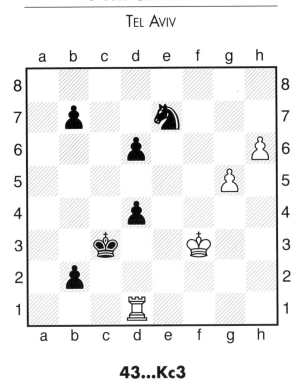

43...Kc3

Analysts' Recommendations: Krush, 43...Kc3;   Paehtz, no recommendation; Felecan, 43...Kc3; Bacrot, 43...Kc3.

Voting Results: 43...Kc3, 4,456; 43...d3, 159; 43...Ng6, 140; 43...Kb3, 75; 43...d5, 56.

Edging closer with the king.

15TH SEPTEMBER

TEL AVIV

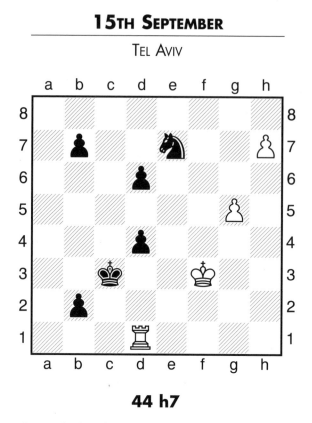

44 h7

This move forces the knight to move over to blockade the pawns and so creates a path for my king directly through to the pawns.

16TH SEPTEMBER

MOSCOW

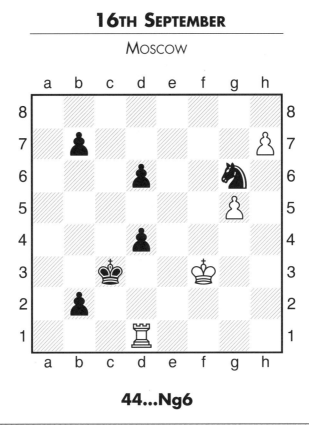

44...Ng6

Analysts' Recommendations: Krush, 44...Ng6; Paehtz, 44...Ng6; Felecan, 44...Ng6; From Bacrot there was again no move recommendation. Following his victory in the French Championship, he went on to play a challenge match against Grandmaster Alexander Belyavsky.

Voting Results: 44...Ng6, 6,902; 44...Kc2, 82; 44...b1(Q), 22; 44...b1(N), 8; 44...d3, 8.

The knight had to stop the h-pawn. Now the route is clear for my king to march up the board.

From a psychological viewpoint this was an interesting moment in the game. Here, I could see that I could force a particular queen ending if I played **45 Rb1**. Black continues 45...d3 46 Ke4 d2 47 Kf5 Kc2 48 Rxb2+ Kxb2 49 Kxg6 d1(Q) 50 h8(Q)+ Kb1. This was indeed the ending we reached in the game. However, I could already see that it was not as promising as I had at first hoped, so why should I lead my opponents into it? By playing **45 Ke4** instead, I wanted to present them with more options in the hope they would play something else. They would still be able to play into this ending, but they could easily be distracted by other continuations, too. In other words, the World would have to decide which particular queen ending offered the best drawing chances, and I wasn't going to present the answer to them on a plate.

Instead of going through the middle with the king, I could also attack the knight from the side: **45 Kg4**. Unfortunately, it would leave my king in a poor position in the resulting queen ending: 45...Kc2 46 Rh1 d3 47 Kh5 Nh8 48 g6 b1Q 49 Rxb1 Kxb1 50 g7 d2 51 gxh8Q d1Q+. If you compare this position with a similar variation later on, then you can see how much better placed Black's king and queen are, and that is enough to hold the draw: 52 Kg6 Qd3+ 53 Kf7 Qc4+! 54 Ke7 Qc7+ 55 Ke6 d5! Black clears the way for more checks, and holds the game.

17TH SEPTEMBER

MOSCOW

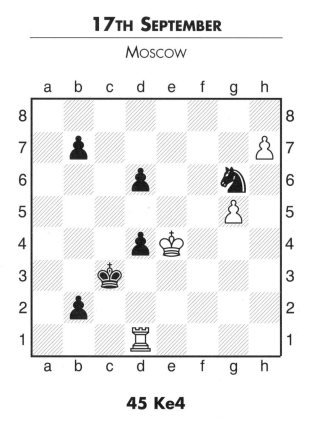

45 Ke4

White's king heads toward the knight.

18TH SEPTEMBER

MOSCOW

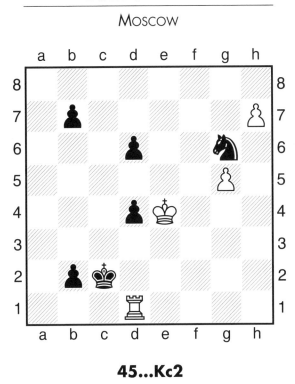

45...Kc2

Analysts' Recommendations: Krush, 45...Kc2; Paehtz, 45...Kc2; Felecan, 45...Kc2; Bacrot: no recommendation, as he continued in a challenge match with Alexander Belyavsky.

Voting Results: 45...Kc2, 5,049; 45...d3, 267; 45...b5, 83; 45...b1(Q), 81; 45...d5, 69.

Forcing the rook to move out of the way, for if **46 Kf5** Kxd1 47 Kxg6 b1(Q)+ even produces a win for Black.

19TH SEPTEMBER

MOSCOW

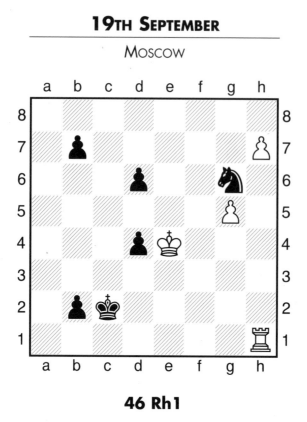

46 Rh1

For safety's sake it is best to move the rook as far away from the king as possible.

Black cannot throw the pawns up in any old fashion. **46...b1(Q)** actually loses: 47 Rxb1 Kxb1 48 Kxd4! and having eliminated the furthest advanced pawn, the king turns back toward the knight and wins the race: 48...b5 49 Ke4 b4 50 Kf5 Nh8 51 g6 b3 52 g7.

20TH SEPTEMBER

MOSCOW

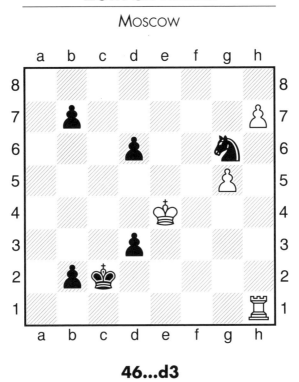

46...d3

> **Analysts' Recommendations:** Krush, 46...d3; Paehtz, 46...d3; Felecan, 46...d3; Bacrot no recommendation as he was still playing the match with Belyavsky.
>
> **Voting Results:** 46...d3, 4,966; 46...b1(Q), 467; 46...Nh8, 53; 46...b5, 25; 46...d5, 22.

There is nothing more I can do to halt the pawns' advance on the queenside; I have to go in with my king to support the pawns.

21ST SEPTEMBER

MOSCOW

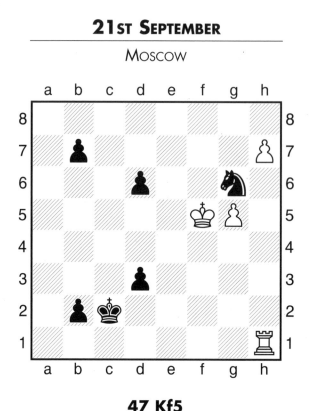

47 Kf5

The World Team had a difficult choice before them. There were three possibilities, all leading to queen endings, but which gave the best drawing chances? From the moment that I played 40 Be3 on September 7, it was fairly clear that this position would arise, so, unluckily for me, my opponents had had two weeks to investigate the different options. Even so, they almost came to the wrong conclusion.

To analyze these queen endings accurately, it is absolutely essential to use a chess computer and, crucially, one with an endgame database. As Boris had access to the most powerful computer of the three of us—Deep Junior —which had an installed database, he took over the lead in our operation, and Yuri's role diminished.

The endgame databases pioneered by Ken Thompson, one of the leading computer scientists in the world, have had a profound effect on chess theory. Using these specialized databases, it is now possible to play any three-, four- and five-piece endgame perfectly. Even some six-piece endings can be managed by the program. The position just needs to be entered into the program, which immediately gives the shortest number of moves to reach a winning position, and exactly how to get there. If it assesses the position as a draw, then it will give the best continuation for the defender.

Thompson spent years working on the databases. Using powerful computers, he generated and cataloged every single position that could occur in the most important three-, four- and five-piece endings (these numbers include kings). The biggest practical problem with the project had been how to store this vast amount of information. Thompson's breakthrough was to divide the board into segments, compute all the positions with the different pieces, then rotate the segment around the board (that's the basic idea). It saved an enormous amount of memory space in the computer and so made the whole task feasible. Of course, the idea of rotating the position worked perfectly for all sets of pieces apart from pawns—after rotating, they would be moving in the wrong direction. Later, Eugene Nalimov, a computer scientist now working for Microsoft, developed Thompson's original ideas by achieving an even greater compression of the existing information, and so managed to add pawns to the database.

With these endgame databases, we now have a definite assessment for every single position with rook and pawn against rook, for example; and crucially, for this game, the same applies for every single position with queen and pawn against queen. In the early 1990s these databases became commercially available, so this fundamental endgame knowledge is now accessible to everyone—including my opponents, of course.

Assessing the position at hand, I considered that, Black could: (a) move the knight; (b) advance the d-pawn; (c) promote the b-pawn. Let's go through each in turn.

a. Move the knight: Checking White's king with the knight would be incorrect, for instance, 47...Nh4+ 48 Kf6, and the h-pawn rolls through faster than Black's pawns. So the only possible option is **47...Nh8**, and the following line represents best play for both sides: 48 g6 d2 49 g7 d1(Q) 50 Rxd1 Kxd1 51 gxh8(Q) b1(Q)+. Black queens with check—a lucky stroke!

At first we believed that this ending was a dead draw—in spite of my pawn on the seventh rank. The problem was that the pawn did nothing to shield the white king from the black queen's checks. But with delicate footwork from the king and queen, we did discover a way to win:

52 Ke6 Qe4+ 53 Kd7 Qa4+ 54 Kc7 d5 (54...b5 55 Kb6! escapes from the checks and wins) 55 Qg7 Qc6+ 56 Kd8 Qd6+ 57 Qd7! Qb8+ 58 Ke7 Qe5+ 59 Kf7 Qf4+ 60 Ke6 Qg4+ 61 Kd6 Qd4 62 Qf5! Qb6+ 63 Kxd5 with a winning position. According to the databases, this is actually a winning position without the pawn on b7; with it, Black's defence is hampered even more as checks from the side are restricted. Here is one fairly typical winning line: 63...Qb5+ 64 Ke6 Qb6+ 65 Ke7 Qb4+ 66 Kf7 Qb3+ 67 Qe6 Qf3+ 68 Ke7 Qc3 69 Qd6+ Ke1 70 Kf7 Qh8 71 Qg3+ Kd1 72 Qg7.

The key moves in this variation are Qd7 and Qf5. These turn out to be the best squares for the queen, allowing White's king to dance around it, so that eventually the checks run out, and then the h-pawn goes through. Black loses in this variation because of the badly placed king on d1: In certain positions, I can block a check by interposing the queen and give check myself, forcing an exchange. With the king in the corner of the board, on b1 for instance, that would be less likely.

For the first ten days of the two-week investigation, the World had not found how I could win—this was their main line. I was getting excited. Back in Tel Aviv the week before, a small group of us had gathered together at the sushi bar at the Hilton hotel. We had drunk a toast with hot sake to the white pawn on h7—then mate in 40, Boris had added. With the help of the endgame database, it would even be possible to announce a forced mate. But the fact that I could avoid this position by playing 45 Rb1 had obviously alerted my opponents, and they discovered how White could win.

b. Advance the d-pawn: 47...d2 48 Kxg6 d1(Q) 49 Rxd1 Kxd1 50 h8(Q) b1(Q)+. Another queen ending, but this time White has a g-pawn, and only on the fifth rank, so, for the World, this continuation was not as dangerous as the far-advanced h-pawn in the previous variation. However, Black's king is once again far from optimally placed on the d1 square, and we considered that White would have reasonable winning chances. A good way to start would be 51 Kg7! Qb2+ 52 Kg8 Qa2+ 53 Kf8 Qa8+ 54 Kg7 Qa1+ 55 Kh7, when Black has already run out of checks due to the king and queen's poor position. We did not consider this ending in too much detail as it was clear that the third option was simply a better version of this variation:

c. Promote the b-pawn: With the following line forced after **47...b1(Q)** 48 Rxb1 Kxb1 49 Kxg6 d2 50h8(Q) d1(Q). Once again, both sides have raced to get a queen. This is very similar to the variation in **b**, but this time Black's king stands on b1 rather than d1. It makes a huge difference to the position. At the side of the board, the king is less vulnerable, and Black's queen is also better placed, unimpeded by its own king.

This might sound hard to believe, but in my chess career I have never had a queen ending of any significant length. Of course, I am familiar with their general theory and strategy, but to play one in practice is quite another matter. Thankfully, the endgame database makes learning much simpler: One can quickly see what the winning positions have in common—and the drawing ones, too.

Above all, I realized that the position of Black's king is the most important factor in the assessment of the position. It stands best around the corner of the board on a1, a2, b1, or b2. It hardly matters where the pawns are. In the variations above it became clear that many positions are winning for me just because the black king is on d1. It is simply a bad square.

We were also amazed to see that there were hardly any winning positions for me if I were left with the g-pawn and Black's king was in the right position on b1 (as in Black's third option above). This was why I was reluctant to force this ending on move 45.

I repeat, the analysis of these positions would have been quite impossible without the help of the database. It meant that every time I reached a position with queen and pawn against queen, I knew for certain whether it was winning for me or drawing. One of Black's strategies in these queen endings would be to give up both remaining pawns so as to make it easier to check my king. That was when the database really came in handy: I knew instantly whether I could get away with capturing the pawns; whether I would have to let them run; or if I had to avoid the variation altogether.

22ND SEPTEMBER

MOSCOW

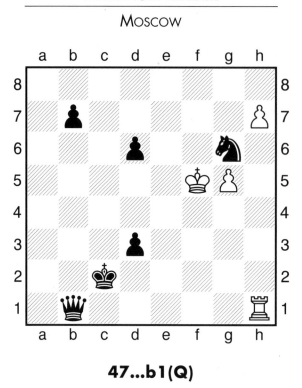

47...b1(Q)

Analysts' Recommendations: Krush, 47...b1 (Q); Paehtz, 47...b1 (Q); Felecan, 47...b1 (Q); Bacrot, 47...b1 (Q).

Voting Results: 47...b1 (Q), 5,534; 47...Nh8, 1,130; 47...d2, 625; 47...Ne7, 82; 47...b1(R), 45.

By now Irina's team had understood which ending gave the best drawing chances, and had been lobbying for it for several days. In the end, the vote wasn't even close. Of course, I have to capture the new queen, and the moves over the next seven days are absolutely forced.

23RD SEPTEMBER

MOSCOW

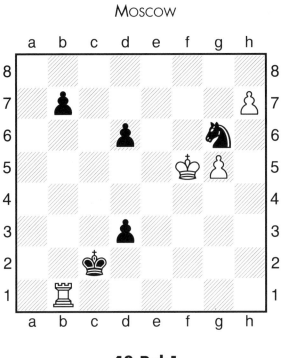

48 Rxb1

I have no choice.

24TH SEPTEMBER

MOSCOW

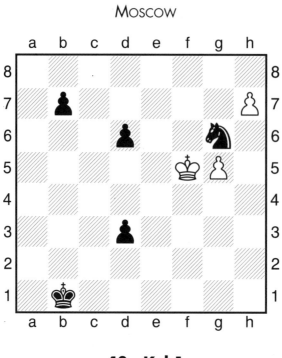

48...Kxb1

Analysts' Recommendations: Krush, 48...Kxb1; Paehtz, 48...Kxb1; Felecan, 48...Kxb1; Bacrot, 48...Kxb1.

Voting Results: 48...Kxb1, 6,012; 48...Nh8, 86; 48...Ne7, 61; 48...d2, 43; 48...Nh4, 32.

The rook must be captured.

25TH SEPTEMBER

MOSCOW

49 Kxg6

The knight must also be captured.

26TH SEPTEMBER

GERMANY

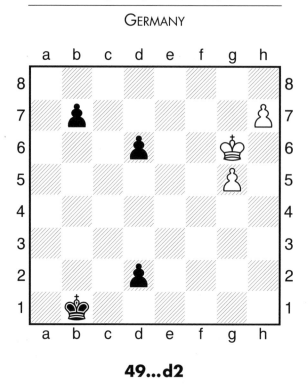

49...d2

Analysts' Recommendations: Krush, 49... d2; Paehtz, 49... d2; Felecan, 49... d2; Bacrot, 49... d2.

Voting Results: 49... d2, 3,610; 49...Ka1, 29; 49...b5, 13; 49...Kc2, 6; 49...d5, 5.

Now both sides stand poised to promote their pawns.

On this day I flew from Moscow to Germany. Systematic AG—a supplier of Internet hardware—had invited me to speak at its launch. It wanted to raise its profile and in so doing boost the IPO of the company. I was happy to do this for a number of reasons: I feel comfortable speaking about new technology; and I also wanted to learn as much as I could for when I would be launching my own online company.

27TH SEPTEMBER

GERMANY

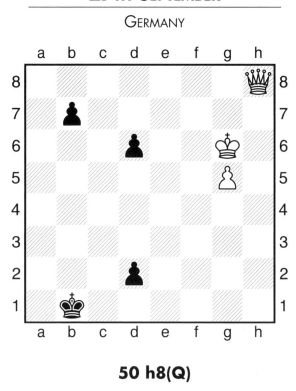

50 h8(Q)

I get a new queen and so does Black.

28TH SEPTEMBER

GERMANY TO MOSCOW

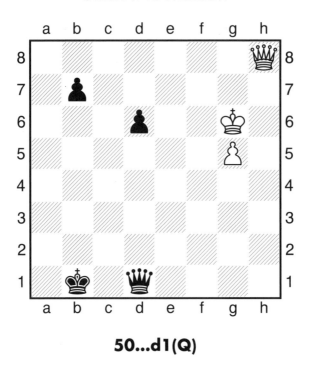

50...d1(Q)

The pawn race has ended in a dead heat. We have arrived at a queen and pawn ending where, in spite of the World's extra pawn, I still have the advantage. Why? The aims in this ending are the same as in most others: to push a pawn to the eighth rank to get another queen. My single pawn has already advanced to the fifth rank, while Black's pawns, a long way from the queening square, isolated, and without proper support, do not represent the same threat. Therefore, the World is fighting for the draw—but it can be achieved with accurate play.

How does the World defend? There are two main ideas: (**a**) Checking. Black's main weapon is to subject my king to a barrage of checks. I have to constantly watch out that my king has enough shelter to prevent a draw by perpetual check. (**b**) Advance the pawns. While I struggle to advance my single pawn, the World attempts to advance its pawns and does so for two reasons. Although Black's pawns are behind in the race, it does no harm to threaten to catch up, and, in addition, those pawns can actually be a hindrance to Black, providing shelter for my king from the checks—particularly the d-pawn, as it is in the center of the board. Advancing the pawns as far as possible removes that cover and makes it more likely that a perpetual check will occur. It is possible that the easiest way for Black to draw is to give up both pawns: In that case one can get an instant assessment from Ken Thompson's database that will also show the perfect way for both sides to play.

That is a very crude outline of the strategy involved in this ending. The play is highly complex. In fact, so complex, that many of the positions that are winning according to the database would be impossible for a human to win against a computer. Remember, with five pieces and fewer, the machine plays perfectly. The winning method is sometimes so complicated that the game no longer has much to do with chess, but geometry.

Of course, to get my g-pawn rolling I have to move my king from in front of the pawn; but if it moves out straightaway, it will be checked right back to where it came from by Black's queen. First, I have to move my queen to a square where it can shield my king.

My original intention was to play **51 Qh5** but, following some excellent work from Boris, it was clear that it would lead nowhere. He had already found the drawing idea when I was in Tel Aviv; it was all on Deep Junior at the Club Kasparov office around September 10th, at the time of Rosh Hashanah, the Jewish new year. The main line runs:

51 Qh5 Qc2+ 52 Kh6 Qc1! This is the best defence, pinning the pawn and so preventing its advance. 53 Qg6+ Ka2 54 Qe6+ d5! Giving up the two pawns is the easiest way to draw. 55 Qxd5+ Ka3 56 Kh5 b5. If the pawn is taken, the database shows that the position is drawn. Instead, 57 g6 Qc3! prevents the pawn from advancing, threatens a check on h3, and prepares to push the b-pawn, given half a chance. Black will not lose: 58 Qxb5 is still a draw according to the database.

This illustrates how valuable the endgame databases are in this kind of position. Once there are only five pieces on the board, the machine takes over; it is only necessary to reach that position and check whether the assessment it gives is in your favor. No further understanding is necessary. Without the use of the database, it would be virtually impossible to defend this position.

When we reached this endgame and I started looking into the database, I was very surprised that the number of winning positions was so small. The conventional wisdom in endings with queen and g-pawn against queen is that the position is nearly always winning when the pawn is on g6 and g7—according to the old analysis of the Russians Yuri Averbakh and Mikhail Botvinnik. But with the help of the database, we found that there were many more drawing positions than were previously imagined and, with the pawn on g5, there is not a single winning position, provided that Black's king is on b1 or a2. And it just so happened that the World's king was on exactly the right spot.

It was clear from the World's analysis that they had also found the right idea against 51 Qh5, so we made a desperate search for an alternative. Nothing worked. Eventually we came up with **51 Qh7**, but we already realized that 51...Ka1 was a dead draw.

29TH SEPTEMBER

MOSCOW

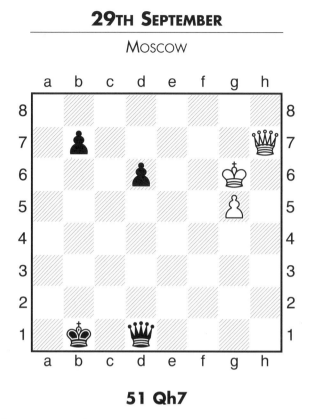

51 Qh7

I wanted to move my king away to uncover a check from the queen. When Black's king moved, then I would have time to advance the pawn or, perhaps even better, bring my queen to a square where it would be able to shield my king from checks, and only then advance the pawn. But it was a vain hope. Frankly, in the time between playing 38 h6 and promoting the pawns, I had given the game up as a draw. I realized that if the World didn't go into the queen ending with the pawn on h7, then I would have no real winning chances. Of course, I kept looking for a way to set a trap, or just cause a little confusion, but I found nothing.

Black's best move was **51...Ka1**, side-stepping my potential queen check.

I could capture the b-pawn, with check even, but it doesn't help me. It merely means that my king has fewer places to shelter, and Black's queen has greater freedom to move. For example:

52 Qg7+ Ka2! 53 Qf7 d5 54 Qf2+ Ka3 55 Kf6 d4 56 g6 d3 57 g7 Qg4 58 Qa7+ Kb2 59 Qb7+ Kc2 60 Qc7+ Kd1 61 Qf7 Qf4+ 62 Kg6 Qg3+; the king has no escape.

Instead of taking the b-pawn, I would probably have transposed back into the variations after 51 Qh5 by playing 52 Qh8+ Kb1 53 Qh5, then eliminated both the World's pawns to reach a theoretically drawn position.

Boris, Yuri, and I had a final discussion. I wanted to gather my loyal comrades and thank them for their help. We had to accept that the game was going to be a draw, but we had hunted well. At least we had the satisfaction of knowing that we had given our best.

I submitted 51 Qh7, resigned to my fate; but on the next afternoon, the World did something rather unexpected.

30TH SEPTEMBER

MOSCOW

51...b5

Analysts' Recommendations: Krush, 51...Ka1; Paehtz, 51...b5; Felecan, 51...d5; Bacrot, no move recommended.

Voting Results: 51...b5, 2,618; 51...Ka1, 2,311; 51...d5, 767; 51...Qd5, 210; 51...Qc2, 179.

For forty moves the voters had loyally followed Irina Krush's recommendations, and now they rejected her. Why?

Perhaps reject is too strong a word—after all, the vote was rather close. There were three plausible moves that caused a split. However, I believe Irina was partly responsible for this divide.

Although she had given 51...Ka1 as her chosen move, in her analysis she also mentioned that 51...b5 was playable. Irina wrote, "...it is possible that 51...b5!? can be considered. I haven't come to a conclusion about this sharp continuation one way or another, and I haven't studied it in much detail, but it may be okay." I think a little complacency had set in on the part of Smart Chess: They had dominated the vote for so long that they forgot about the need to keep canvassing for support. Because Irina failed to give a strong, unequivocal recommendation, there was indecision within the World Team that led to a split vote—and a poor move was chosen.

Moreover, moving the b-pawn two squares in its march to the eighth rank is somehow a more "natural" move for most chess players than the more subtle 51...Ka1, which, after all, leaves the b-pawn *en prise* (even though its capture wasn't to be feared). I think that also partly explains the popularity of the move amongst the World Team.

Although 51...b5 isn't a bad move, it is certainly not as good as 51...Ka1. When the move appeared, I immediately called Yuri and Boris. "The World Team ignored Irina. I think Smart Chess is getting complacent. Maybe we have a chance—let's work again."

It was around here that I established certain ground rules for the ending: (1) the key square for White's queen is d4; (2) in moving out from in front of the g-pawn, White's king must go to f6 and toward the center, not to the h-file; (3) Black's pawn must be stopped on d5—on that square it impedes the mobility of Black's queen; (4) and the best square for the Black king is usually on b1.

While precise calculation was needed at all times in this ending, I believe it certainly helped us in our analysis to have these guidelines. It gave us something to adhere to as we pored over the mass of variations unfolding in front of us.

1st October

Moscow

52 Kf6+

I moved my king out of the way, uncovering a check from the queen on h7. After Black's king moved out of check, I wanted to reposition my queen to a better square so that it could shield my king from checks (on h7 it is doing nothing). Queens normally function best in the center of the board where they can exert the most influence. Unfortunately, we discovered that with best defense, Black should still be holding the draw.

52...Kc1 was the best move—it avoids a check when White's queen moves to d4. Although I come close to winning, with accurate play, Black is able to hold the draw: 53 g6 Qf3+ (53...b4? 54 Qh6+ Kb1 55 g7 Qf3+ 56 Ke6, and the king is going to find cover) 54 Ke7 Qe4+ 55 Kd7, and again, instead of pushing the b-pawn, it is best to keep checking: 55...Qb7+ 56 Kxd6 Qb6+ 57 Kd5 Qd8+ 58 Kc6 Qe8+ (58...Qa8+? 59 Kb6 Qb8+ 60 Qb7 with chances) 59 Kb7 Qe4+ 60 Kb8 Qe8+ 61 Ka7 Qe3+ 62 Ka6 Qe6+. White is getting nowhere—the queen on h7 is very poorly placed.

Instead of 53 g6 I could try to redeploy my queen to a better square, but that is also insufficient to win: 53 Qe4 b4! 54 Qxb4, and now here is the trick, Black plays 54...Qf3+ 55 Kg7 d5, and I can play 56 Qd4, but Black just plays 56...Qe4, forcing my queen from the key square. This is crucial—compare this with what happened in the game where my queen came to d4 with check. And 56 g6 is met by 56...d4. If White captures the pawn then a drawn position arises—according to the endgame database. A useful tool, to put it mildly.

2ND OCTOBER

MOSCOW

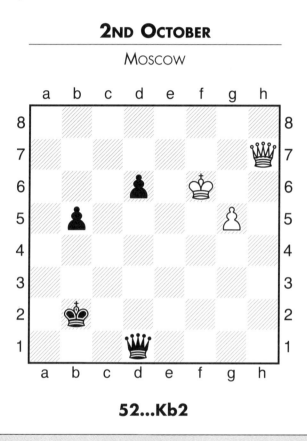

52...Kb2

Analysts' Recommendations: Krush, 52...Kc1; Paehtz, 52...Kb2; Felecan, 52...Kb2; Bacrot, 52...Ka1.

Voting Results: 52...Kb2, 2,340; 52...Kc1, 2,226; 52...Ka1, 544; 52...Qc2, 235; 52...Ka2, 103.

Extraordinary. The vote narrowly went against Irina again. How did that happen? It was a combination of factors of course, a loss of a sense of danger, chiefly, but it was surely significant that the St. Petersburg GM school gave 52...Kb2 as their recommendation.

After 52...Kb2, even if the position were still drawn, I felt that I was extremely close to winning.

Nevertheless, at this point I had a tough decision before me. **53 Qh2+** and **53 Qe4** were the most plausible options, but which was best? I could be throwing away the win if I played the wrong move. It was like stepping through a minefield.

I was very tempted by 53 Qe4, a classic centralizing move. There was one crucial variation where I could get my pawn right to the seventh rank, but it seemed impossible to get it that one vital step further: 53...Qf1+ 54 Qf5 Qc4 55 g6 b4 56 g7 b3. And now what? The more I looked, the more it seemed I was going around in circles. Boris was on holiday for a few days, but I called Shay Bushinsky, Deep Junior's creator, and asked him to feed this position to his protégé. I called back in one hour. "Junior doesn't see a win," Shay said. Then it had to be a draw. If this monster of a chess computer couldn't promote the pawn in that time, then my feeling was that it simply couldn't be done. But who knows? Perhaps in this complex position it needed just a little more time—but we didn't have it. Incidentally, afterward Boris investigated 53 Qe4 Qb3, another defense, and could not find a win for White.

Anyway, all this is moot. I decided to go for the other move.

3RD OCTOBER

MOSCOW

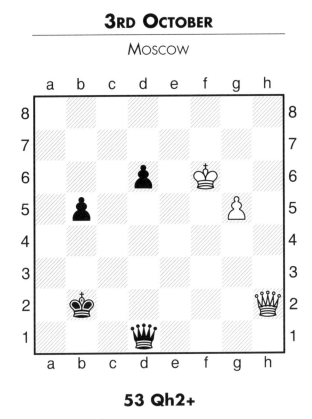

53 Qh2+

This isn't a wonderful square for the queen, but it is passing through on its way to somewhere better. Black's king has several squares to choose from, but most are poor, as they allow my queen more checking options. I only considered that Black's king would go to a1.

4TH OCTOBER

MOSCOW

53...Ka1

Having twice snubbed Irina's recommendation, the voters returned to her for this move. This time they absolutely had to. And, once again, I was faced with a very difficult decision; so difficult that in the end I really just made an educated guess. I couldn't yet advance my pawn, as my queen was too poorly placed—my king would be checked mercilessly. Therefore my move was going to be either **54 Qf4** or **54 Qf2**, both of which shielded my king from checks, but I just couldn't work out which was better. Boris and Deep Junior couldn't give me any firm advice: The situation was so complex that they hadn't been able to come to any conclusions. (Incidentally, Smart Chess now considers that 54 Qf2 would have been a more promising try for White).

The deadline to submit my move to Microsoft was 5 AM Moscow time. I sat in my study at home until 4 AM, unable to reach a decision. It was the longest I had spent on one of my moves in this game. In the end, it was one single variation that persuaded me how to play:

After 54 Qf4 I first thought that Black was drawing with 54...Qd3 55 g6 Qc3+ 56 Kf7 Qc7 57 Kf8 (the best move) 57...Qb8+ 58 Kg7 b4 59 Kh7 b3, and now after 60 g7 Qa7. After 61 Kh8 b2 62 g8(Q) b1(Q) both sides have two queens but there is no mating attack, it is just a draw.

However, instead of 60 g7, I found a beautiful way to win: 60 Qa4+ Kb2 61 g7 Qb7 and now a great move 62 Qh4! shielding the king on the h-file. 62...Ka3 63 Kh8 b2 64 Qg3+. Now if 64...Qb3 I exchange and queen on g8 with check, so: 64...Ka4 65 Qf4+. Black cannot interpose on b4 as I exchange, get a new queen with g8, then win Black's new queen with Qb8+. Therefore, 65...Ka5, but White wins by 66 Qf5+ Ka4 (if 66...d5 67 g8Q—Black's queening square is covered) 67 g8Q Qh1+ 68 Kg7 Qg2+ 69 Kf7 Qb7+ 70 Kf6 b1Q 71 Qc4+ Q1b4 72 Qfc2+, mate follows rapidly.

Discovering this line gave me confidence. I decided that 54 Qf4 was the right way to go.

5TH OCTOBER

MOSCOW

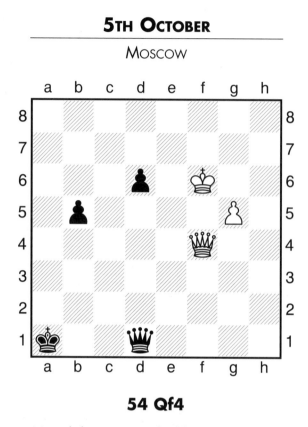

54 Qf4

Having repositioned the queen to shield my king, I am at last ready to advance my pawn.

6TH OCTOBER

MOSCOW TO LOS ANGELES

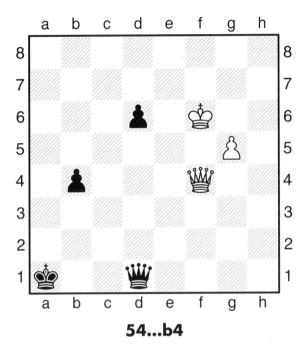

54...b4

> **Analysts' Recommendations:** Krush, 54...b4; Paehtz, 54...Qd3; Felecan, 54...Qd3; Bacrot, 54...Qd5.
>
> **Voting Results:** 54...b4, 3,557; 54...Qd3, 1,043; 54...Qd5, 801; 54...d5, 280; 54...Qa4, 38.

I wasn't pleased to see 54...b4. I had to take the pawn and that meant we were one step closer to a position where the five-piece database would come into play. In other words, we were getting to a situation where my opponents could rely on someone else's analysis rather than having to think for themselves.

My feeling at the time was that 54...b4 was a strong move. The pawn is sacrificed so as to deflect my queen from its powerful central position, allowing Black's queen to occupy a better square. From there it can harass my king, and so slow the advance of my pawn. The queen is the most powerful piece on the board, but if it does not get into a position where it can demonstrate that power, then its value diminishes.

However, subsequently it was proved that 54...b4 was actually Black's final and decisive mistake—and isn't it ironic that Irina, as the only analyst to recommend the move, was responsible for it. After the game, as an extension of the five-piece endgame databases, Peter Karrer, a Swiss player who had been active on the bulletin boards for the World Team, generated some databases for this particular six-piece endgame with Black d- and White g-pawns, and queens and kings. Now it is not a matter of opinion whether the position is winning or drawing, we simply know the truth.

According to his research, it turns out that Etienne Bacrot's suggestion of 54...Qd5 is the final chance for the World Team to save the game—a move that, frankly, we did not have time to consider at all. The idea is that after 55 g6, Black counters with 55...b4! If the pawn is captured, then ...Qe5+ is a perpetual. Variations are long and complex and I have no desire to go into them here. I am happy to stand by the claim of analysts at the Smart Chess site that 54...Qd5 leads to a draw.

On the previous Saturday I had received a phone call from Owen Williams about appearing in a TV commercial for Alta Vista, an Internet search engine. Three days later I was on a plane over the Pole bound for Los Angeles.

The shoot was a success. I got on well with the director, Joe Pytka—one of the best in the business—perhaps because we are both perfectionists. The scene was a simultaneous display: there were twenty-six boards, filled by actors who had little idea about the game of chess, so we had fun with continuity and authenticity. But there was one familiar face in the crowd. Who knows how he got to be there, but standing behind one of the "players" was the round figure of one of the great characters in the chess world, Grandmaster Eduard Gufeld, now a resident of Los Angeles.

I have known "Goofy" since I won the Soviet Junior Championship in 1976. He was there as trainer to Maya Chiburdanidze—who won the girls championship played at the same time. At a party Goofy hosted after the championships were over, he proposed a toast to Maya and myself. He declared that she would become women's World Champion in 1978 and that I would be World Champion in 1984. He was absolutely correct in the case of Maya, and only one year off schedule with me.

A couple of years later, he gave me some advice—in his inimitable style—for which I will always be grateful. It was 1978 and I had just made fifty percent in my first Soviet Championship. Once again, Gufeld was throwing a party. He told me, "Garry, how can you play the Caro-Kann?" (my main weapon against 1 e4 at that time). "You look like one of the Mafiosi—you must play the Sicilian!" And the rest is history.

7TH OCTOBER

LOS ANGELES

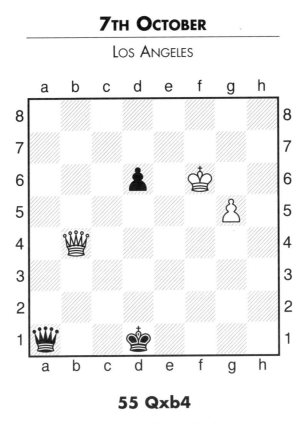

55 Qxb4

I could not allow the b-pawn to advance further, so this move was forced.

8TH OCTOBER

LOS ANGELES TO NEW YORK

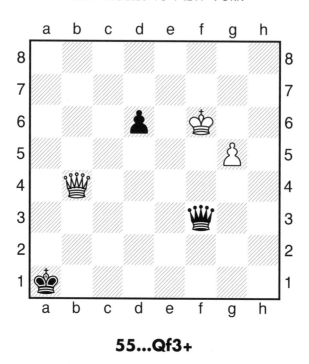

55...Qf3+

Analysts' Recommendations: Krush, 55...Qf3+; Paehtz, 55...Qf3+; Felecan, 55...Qf3+; Bacrot, 55...Qf3+.

Voting Results: 55...Qf3+, 5,356; 55...d5, 169; 55...Qd4, 159; 56...Qe1, 151; 56...Qa4, 137.

This was the idea behind the pawn sacrifice: Having deflected my queen from its strong position, Black's queen immediately takes its place, checking my king, which must move in front of the g-pawn. For instance, if I try **56 Ke7**, then 56...Qe3+ forces it to return to protect the pawn.

9TH OCTOBER

NEW YORK

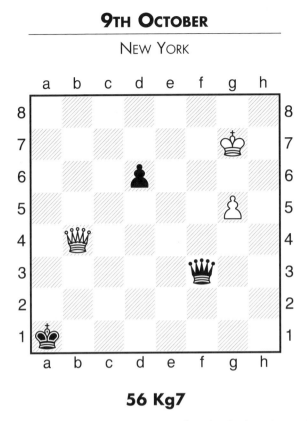

56 Kg7

At least on this square, my king cannot be checked again, and I am "threatening" to advance my pawn.

I managed to combine my trip to Los Angeles with a stay in New York. I was there for more meetings about the setting up of KasparovChess Online, not an easy operation to coordinate. The company was going to be a U.S. corporation, with the management team based in New York; Tel Aviv would take care of the technical side of the operation; and the principal chess office would be in Moscow.

I was also able to visit my daughter from my first marriage, Polina. Now 7 years old, she lives with her mother in New Jersey. This was the first time that I had received full visiting rights, so she was able to stay overnight with me. Of course, I was rather anxious about how things would turn out, but it went just fine; we got on well. It is curious how she switches back and forth between speaking Russian and English. The territory is very clearly divided: When she is at home or with me, she speaks Russian, even when other people are around who only speak English. At other times, she is perfectly comfortable speaking English.

10TH OCTOBER

NEW YORK

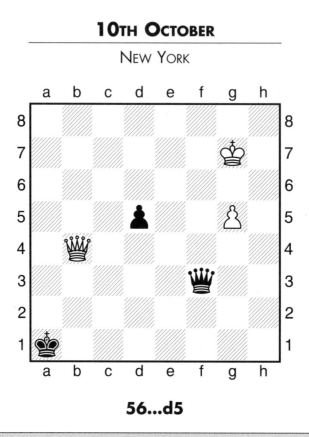

56...d5

I was amazed that none of the analysts recommended 56...Qe3. As they all went for 56...d5 I didn't continue my research into the queen move, but still, I was in no doubt that it was Black's best chance. As far as I was concerned, it was the only way that the sacrifice of the pawn with 54...b4 could be justified. By omitting ...Qe3, Black loses control of the d4 square, allowing my queen to return to its ideal position, blockading the pawn. Additionally, from a positional viewpoint, the pawn stands poorly on d5. It prevents Black's queen from utilizing the long diagonal (for instance, if Black's queen is on h1, g2 or f3, then it cannot cut across to b7); and in variations where my king lands on g8, the pawn shields it from checks along another important diagonal.

Subsequently, it was proved by Peter Karrer that after 56...Qe3, White is still winning, but only after generating the solution from endgame databases. For example: 57 Qa5+ Kb2 58 Qb5+ Ka1 59 g6 d5 60 Qa6+ Kb1 61 Qf1+ Ka2 62 Qg2+ Ka3 63 Kh7 Qd3 64 Kh8 Qf5 65 Qg3+ Ka4 66 Qh4+ d4 67 g7 Qe5 68 Qg4 Kb3 69 Kh7 Qh2+ 70 Kg6 Qd6+ 71 Kh5 Qe5+ 72 Kh4 wins.

At the time we were quite uncertain whether the position was winning: 56...Qe3 felt like the correct move.

After 56...d5, if I advance my pawn straightaway, **57 g6**, then Black would be able to draw by playing 57...d4. The position after the pawn is captured is a draw according to the five-piece database; and if it isn't captured, then the pawn is simply too close to the queening square. I would have no real advantage. However, I can play **57 Qd4+**, blockading the pawn. My intuition told me that the position was now winning for me.

11TH OCTOBER

NEW YORK

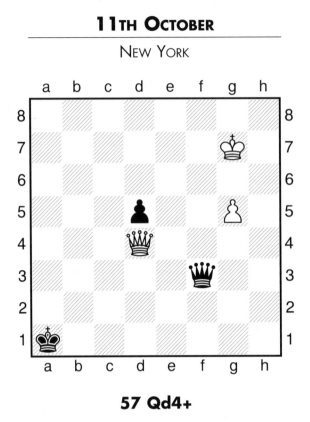

57 Qd4+

The queen arrives on the perfect square, and with a check, so I gain a move. One might imagine that analyzing a position with just a few pieces would be a fairly straightforward matter. Nothing could be further from reality. As both kings have so little cover, they are vulnerable to checks. In some variations, my king is driven right across to the other side of the board, seemingly powerless to escape, but returns along a slightly different path to elude Black's queen, finally resulting in the g-pawn marching home. In other scenarios, a similar situation only results in a draw—and working out where the difference lies seemingly defies logic. It is impossible to rely only on "feeling" here. Calculations must be carried through until a position is reached that is definitely drawing or winning. With each move often offering more than one plausible continuation, it is not difficult to see that a line twenty moves deep can quickly branch out into a tangled mass of complex variations that could blow one's mind.

Therefore, to aid and simplify our task, Boris identified a set of positions we knew were definitely winning for me, all with the pawn on either d5 or d4. There were seventeen in total. That in itself was a remarkable achievement—

Boris spent countless hours working on these positions. They acted like guideposts in the middle of a maze: We could aim for them knowing that we were on exactly the right path. For instance, one of those positions was: White queen on f4; White king on g4; White pawn on g6, Black queen on e7, Black king on c2, Black pawn on d5. With White to move, this position is winning.

Constructing these seventeen positions not only gave some structure to our work but also helped Deep Junior in its analysis. It only needed to reach one of these positions, or one from the endgame database, to reach an immediate conclusion, so it did not need to investigate further, and that meant it could move on to explore other variations.

When I was traveling, away from my computer with the endgame database, the only way I could analyze properly was to memorize these positions; then at least I could understand what Boris was talking about over the phone. We would reach a position in which I wouldn't have the slightest idea how I should go about winning, but at least I knew it was possible.

12TH OCTOBER

NEW YORK

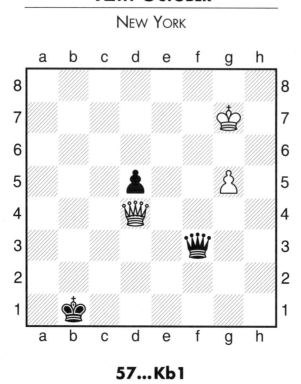

57...Kb1

There can be no argument with this move, this is the best square for the king. Instead, on a2 the king would stand on the diagonal leading to the g-pawn's queening square. That would be too risky. When I queened it would be with check, which would give me, in certain variations, a decisive extra tempo.

13TH OCTOBER

NEW YORK

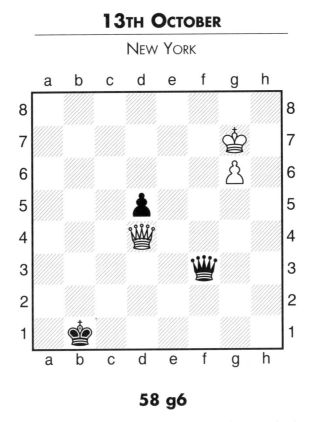

58 g6

Having brought my queen to its best square, the time had come to advance my pawn toward the eighth rank.

In this position Black must attempt to bring the queen back into play to check White's king. There are two plausible ways of doing this, one much better than the other, though I didn't believe that either was sufficient to hold the game. For about a week Irina's team mainly analyzed **58...Qe4**. It took them some time to realize that the move would lose quite simply (at least by computer standards). Only in the last couple of days before this vote did Irina change her mind and start to recommend **58...Qf5**—Khalifman's suggestion and the best try—in this position.

As usual, I had submitted my move, 58 g6, before my deadline of 6 PM PST (Pacific Standard Time) on Wednesday, October 13th. I actually sent it in early, so the four analysts received my move at 3PM PST. They then had until 6 AM PST the following morning to submit their move recommendation to Microsoft. It was business as usual.

14TH OCTOBER

NEW YORK TO WASHINGTON, D.C., TO NEW YORK

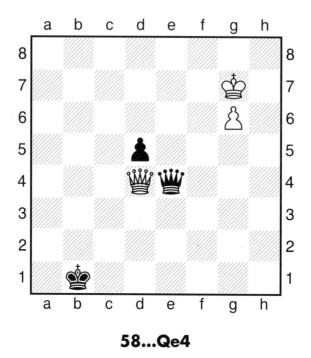

58...Qe4

Analysts' Recommendations: Krush, recommendation not received; Paehtz, 58...Qe4; Felecan, 58...Qf5; Bacrot, 58...Qe4.

Voting Results: Draw offer 4,854; 58...Qe4, 3,922; 58...Qf5, 3,527; 58...Qh1 204; 58...Kc2, 75; 58...Qb3, 54.

Three of the analysts sent Microsoft their recommendations by the 6 AM PST deadline. However, apparently due to an e-mail server problem, Irina had received my move late. Because of that, she only managed to submit her recommendation after she returned from school, at 12:20 PM PST, several hours after the 6 AM PST deadline, and after voting had already begun. In fact, due to another technical glitch, her e-mail was not received by Microsoft until 4 PM PST, in other words, ten hours late. Irina's move recommendation, therefore, was not accepted for posting to the game's website. It had happened before with the other analysts, and Microsoft felt there was no need to make an exception for her. As Eddie Ranchigoda later explained, "After 4 PM we generally do not have resources to update the site unless an emergency occurs."

As Elisabeth and Etienne had recommended 58...Qe4 (Elisabeth's move was even accompanied by a draw offer), it won the vote—narrowly. It is quite possible that had Irina's recommendation been posted as usual, then **58...Qf5** would have been the majority move. After all, since the World team went their own way at moves 51 and 52, she had managed to win back the voters to her cause.

Irina and her supporters were extremely upset. They felt that a chance for a draw had been unfairly taken from them. However, it seems to me that Irina and Smart Chess were as much responsible for this turn of events as anyone or anything else.

Irina could have sent her recommendation in anyway, as it was fairly clear what my move was going to be. Or she could have asked her managers at Smart Chess to take care of the problem. And why no one picked up a telephone to talk through the situation is a mystery to me. With hindsight, all this becomes clear. The point is, Smart Chess must have assumed that Microsoft would accept Irina's move, even if it was sent in late. A certain complacency had set in.

The Microsoft management squarely rejected calls from the bulletin boards and chat rooms for the vote to be held again. This was Eddie Ranchigoda's response on one of the game site's regular chats.

"Microsoft has remained completely objective throughout this event. Although we root for the World Team to succeed, we have tried to create an event that is a fair competition for both sides. To suspend a vote and order a revote when there were no technical abnormalities simply because the winning vote may be a losing vote [sic] would be completely contradictory to this objectivity."

The whole argument seemed irrelevant to me. Our analysis led us to believe that, while more difficult, we were also winning after **58...Qf5**, and this was later confirmed by Peter Karrer's six-piece database. Boris had realized some time before that this was the only plausible defense. Our first intention was to play 59 Qb6+. Here we found wins against all moves except 59...Kc1. However, it did give us some good ideas on how to play the position.

Then we discovered the crucial Zugzwang position after 59 Kh6 Qe6.

The trick here is to reach this same position, but with Black to move instead of White. So White plays 60 Qd1+ Kb2 61 Qd2+ Kb1 62 Qd4. It is the same position as before, but this time it is Black to move. The point is that Black's king and queen already stand on their best squares, so whatever move is made, the defensive position is compromised. Once again, variations are numerous and complicated, and I do not wish to give a comprehensive survey of lines here. There is nothing more to prove as all parties involved agree that this is a winning position for White. Let me just give one "typical" winning line. The most stubborn move for Black here is 62...Ka2. (On other squares, the king is more vulnerable or gets in the way of Black's queen.) 63 Kg5 Qe7+ 64 Qf6 Qe3+ 65 Qf4 Qg1+ (65...Qe7+ 66 Kh6 Qe6 67 Qf3! is very neat, Black has no defense to Kh7 and g7) 66 Kf6 Qb6+ 67 Kf7 Qb7+ 68 Ke6 Qc8+ 69 Kf6 Qd8+ 70 Kf5 Qc8+ 71 Kg5 Qc3 72 Qh2+ Ka1 73 Qe2 Kb1 74 Qf2 Qc1+ 75 Kg4 Qc3 76 Qf1+ Kb2 77 Kf5 Qc7 78 Qe2+ Kb1 79 Qd3+ Ka2 80 Qa6+ Kb2 81 Qe6 Ka2 82 Qf7 Qc2+ 83 Ke6 Qe2+ 84 Kxd5. This position is a win, according to the five-piece database, defying human logic. How should one begin to explain White's queen moves on the seventy-third and seventy-fourth moves?

All in all, this was a bizarre day for me. I had been invited to Washington, D.C., by Chris Cox, Congressman for Orange County, California, to speak to the policy board of the House Leadership Committee. I have known Chris since 1991 when I briefly became involved in politics. As chairman of the leadership committee, he is one of the most influential members of Congress. Chris has always shown a keen interest in Russian politics: He was in Moscow for the last two presidential elections, and we met up on both occasions (in 1996, I even acted as his interpreter on a radio show for him).

I had a 9:15 AM flight from LaGuardia airport to Washington, D.C. I woke early, had time for a proper breakfast, and made it to the airport with a little time to spare. Unfortunately, I hadn't realized that it was necessary to have photo identification to get onto the flight. So it was back to the Plaza to pick up my passport, then a quick turn around to catch the next shuttle. It was on the second trip to the airport that I received news from my cousin Yevgeny in Moscow that 58...Qe4 had been played. I had time for a quick word with Boris in Israel before getting on the plane. Then it was lunch and a talk in Washington with the committee, followed by a quick tour of the House before heading back to the airport for a 5:30 PM flight. It turned out that there were weather problems in La Guardia, so Owen and I headed back into town to catch a train back to New York instead. We arrived into the Pennsylvania Station at around 10 PM. There, we were greeted by an enormous crowd of people—flooding out of Madison Square Garden from a New York Rangers ice hockey game. There wasn't a spare taxi cab in sight, and it was absolutely freezing. Some days just don't run smoothly. We had to think like New Yorkers. We ducked across the street; a few dollars changed hands with a hotel doorman; and in an instant we had a cab.

15TH OCTOBER

NEW YORK

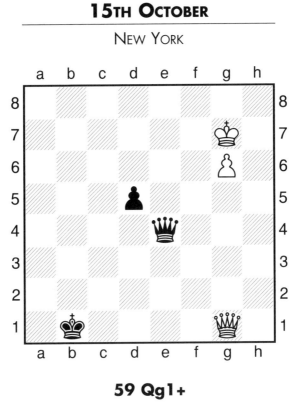

59 Qg1+

By bouncing off the back rank with check, I can bring my queen to the f2 square without losing time. On the f-file, the queen will shield my king when it moves out from in front of the pawn.

16TH OCTOBER

LONDON

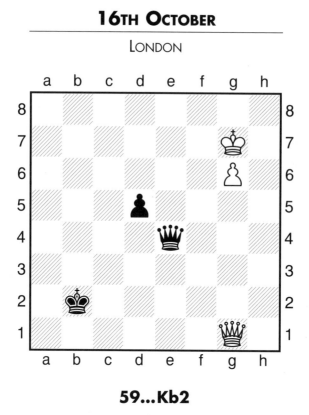

59...Kb2

Analysts' Recommendations: Krush, no recommendation; Paehtz, 59...Kc2; Felecan, 59...Kb2; Bacrot, 59...Kb2.

Voting Results: 59...Kb2, 1,667; 59...Kc2, 1,356; Draw, 93; 59...Ka2, 47.

For this move, Irina decided not to give a specific recommendation. Instead she gave an analysis of the three most plausible options, concluding in each case that Black was lost. She finished by mentioning a fourth possibility:

"Finally, we should not forget: 59...Qe1, when after 60 Qxe1+, White wins as Black's queen has left the game."

On the bulletin boards this was taken to mean that Irina was looking for the World to give up its queen—a gesture to symbolize her departure from the game. The strength of feeling was such that many people must have voted for 59...Qe1, but it was also clear at Microsoft that some "ballot stuffing" had taken place: Multiple votes had been received from the same e-mail addresses.

This issue had already surfaced a few days before on the bulletin boards when it had been revealed how to manipulate the system by sending in multiple votes. In Seattle the situation had been closely monitored, but the effect of ballot stuffing had been negligible; certainly not enough to change the results of any votes. When designing the game, Microsoft had decided against a more secure voting mechanism, such as e-mail notification and confirmation by code word, as it would have required voters to carry out several cumbersome steps, slowing the whole procedure and discouraging many from participating. Throughout the game, participants had simply been relied on not to cheat—and they had not done so in any significant numbers until now. This was Microsoft's response:

"The spirit of Kasparov vs. The World has been compromised by widespread 'ballot stuffing' in favor of 59...Qe1. To rectify the situation, the Gaming Zone disqualified the Qe1 move. We hope that sportsmanlike conduct will return so that future votes are not affected by ballot stuffing. We encourage World Team members to cast just one vote in favor of their selected move. We also wish to clarify that Ms. Krush's recommendation for move 58 was received by us over ten hours late; due, in part, to server delay. As you may remember, there have been other instances when analysts recommendations were not posted to the site; we want to point out that late receipt of the recommendation is the reason for the recommendation not being posted, in this case and in the others."

—Diane McDade, PR manager, Microsoft

Shortly after this, Irina declared that as she considered the game position to be lost, she would play no further part in the proceedings. Therefore, no further move recommendations were received from Irina.

17TH OCTOBER

LONDON

60 Qf2+

The queen arrives where I want it on the f-file, again, with a check, so I
don't lose time.

18TH OCTOBER

LONDON

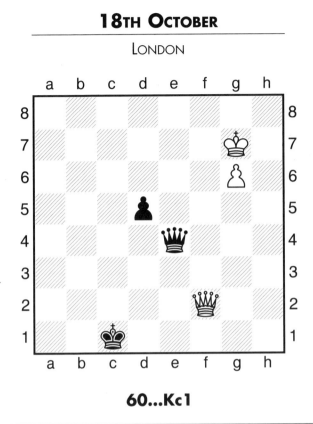

60...Kc1

Analysts' Recommendations: Krush, no recommendation; Paehtz, 60...Kc1; Felecan, 60...Ka1; Bacrot, no recommendation.

Voting Results: 60...Kc1, 1,836; draw offer, 1,391; resign, 1391; 60...Kc3, 1307; 60...Qc2, 791.

The win was now just a matter of time. Black's best move, 60...Kc3, would have prolonged the game, but not more; it was already beyond saving. A couple of moves ago, the World had offered a draw; and now "resigns" was quickly gaining support in the vote.

19TH OCTOBER

LONDON

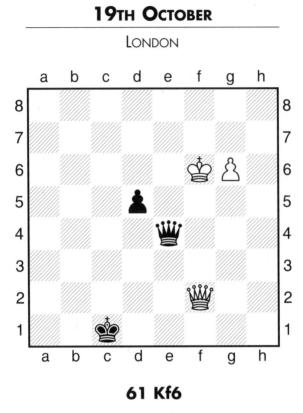

61 Kf6

The king emerges from in front of the pawn safely, as Black's queen is unable to give any checks. And that means the pawn can advance on the next turn.

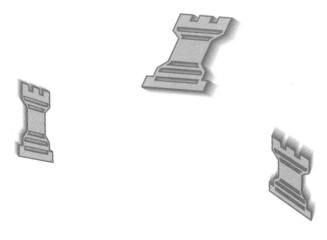

20TH OCTOBER

LONDON

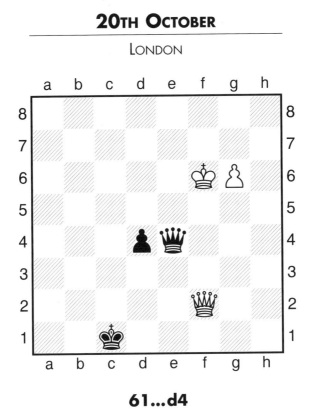

61...d4

Analysts' Recommendations: Krush, no recommendation; Paehtz, 61...d4; Felecan, Resign; Bacrot, 61...d4.

Voting Results: 61...d4, 3,495; resign, 2,050; 61...Qe8, 155; 61...Qc2, 63; 61...Qg6, 54.

Black's pawn push comes too late.

21ST OCTOBER

LONDON

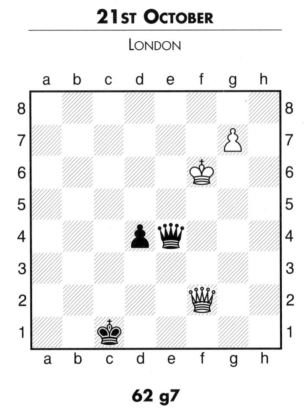

62 g7

The pawn cannot be prevented from queening—its coronation can only be delayed by a series of Black checks to my king. It takes a little time, but it is a relatively simple task for me to find a path out of the checks.

Irina had already departed from the game, Florin had recommended resigning on the last move, and now it was Elisabeth's turn to announce her resignation. I was actually hoping that the World would continue for a few more days so that I could announce a forced mate, but, considering that the majority of the analysts had now abandoned the struggle, the result of the next vote was predictable.

RESIGNS, 22ND OCTOBER

LONDON

> **Voting Results:** resign, 3,118; 62...Qc6, 1,961; 62...d3, 317; 62...Qd5, 194; 62...Qg4, 119.

At noon Pacific Standard Time—8 PM where I was in London—Microsoft posted the results of the final vote. I felt that as "resigns" had only just crept over the 50 percent needed for it to be carried, it was only right that I give a final variation demonstrating the way to win. In fact, as Deep Junior had an installed endgame database, it was not only possible to give the quickest number of moves to force the promotion of the pawn, but from there it could actually give the shortest number of moves to force checkmate. Therefore, I was able to announce a forced mate in twenty-five moves:

62...Qc6+ 63 Kg5 Qd5+ 64 Qf5 Qg2+ 65 Qg4 Qd5+ 66 Kh4! Qg8

(Instead if 66...Qh1+ 67 Kg3 Qe1+ 68 Kf4 Qd2+ 69 Kf5 Qc2+ 70 Kg5 Qc5+ 71 Kh4 d3 72 g8(Q) Qf2+ 73 Qg3 Qf6+ 74 Kg4 Qd4+ 75 Kh3 Kb2 76 Qg2+ Kc1 77 Qh1+ Kd2 78 Qa2+ Ke3 79 Qe1+ Kf4 80 Qf7+ Kg5 81 Qd2+ Qe3+ 82 Qxe3 mate)

67 Qf4+ Kc2 68 Qf8 Qh7+ 69 Kg5 Qh2 70 g8(Q).

Once the pawn promotes to a queen, this is, of course, the end for Black, but it is nice to be able to go to checkmate.

70...Qg3+ 71 Kf5 Qf3+ 72 Ke6 Qb3+ 73 Kd6 Qb4+ 74 Ke5 Qe1+ 75 Kxd4.

Now it's mate in twelve. For example:

75...Qa1+ 76 Ke4 Qa4+ 77 Ke3 Qa7+ 78 Kf3 Qb7+ 79 Kg3 Qc7+ 80 Qf4 Qxf4+ 81 Kxf4 Kd3 82 Qb3+ Kd4 83 Qb5 Kc3 84 Ke3 Kc2 85 Qb4 Kc1 86 Kd3 Kd1 87 Qd2 mate. If Black deviates from this line then checkmate arrives even sooner.

When the game was over, I was immediately asked if I would be willing to repeat the event. I was hesitant not because I would not relish a new challenge but because we could play a thousand times over and never re-create such an extraordinary game as this. I believe Kasparov vs. the World was one of the greatest games of chess ever played. But I will let you be the judge of that. . .

Garry Kasparov

World Champion